LORI G

Shackles

For Jordan and Justin,
My World Changers

Acknowledgements

I would like to thank my husband, Ryan, for his unwavering and unconditional love. His sacrifices, "dying to himself daily," and ability to always assume positive intent has transformed the way I view life and in turn shown me what it is to truly love someone. I am so thankful that the Lord brought me such a perfect gift. Thank you for supporting me in everything I put my hands to. I love you!

I would like to extend a special thank you to my children, Jordan and Justin. Your willingness to always see the good in me and support of everything I do have allowed me to follow God's calling in my life. Your patience as I went through each process proves God's goodness and grace. To see you both smile and thriving in life truly makes my heart happy. My proudest accomplishment in life is being your mama!

I would like to thank and honor my parents, Bill and Shirley Parsley, for the godly example they display in everything they do. They masterfully lead our entire family with a humble, kind, giving, nurturing manner that has created a stability that no Devil in Hell can shake. Through their example and their personal relationship with the Lord, they have tirelessly counseled and prayed for each family member, proving themselves to be an iconic patriarch and matriarch of our family. I love you both so much!

A huge shout out to Lisa and Ruth...my sisters, my first friends, my forever best friends. You have taught me so much about myself and I am the person I am today because of you. Your willingness to always listen and to be honest (even when it was not the popular opinion) has strengthened our bond beyond what I could have ever imagined.

Rutie, BSGO, you are the best big sister a person could ever hope for! Patsa Lou, thank you for the constant cheerleading and being a perfect example of a Proverbs 31 woman, you gave me something to strive for...here is the front row seat you requested twelve years ago. I love you both!

I would like to say an enormous "thank you" to my entire family, my tribe. I could write another book based on your acts of kindness, support, and coveted prayers on my behalf. Every single one of you is a piece to this puzzle and it wouldn't be complete without you! I am most blessed to have a tribe like you.

Also, I would like to extend a huge thank you to Gail Dudley. Your coaching, advice, and expertise on this project is what enabled me to bring forth my entire vision for Shackles. Thank you!

TABLE OF CONTENTS

INTRODUCTION

———————

"I ONCE WAS LOST, BUT NOW I'M FOUND" has a new meaning to me. I remember so clearly after being away from the Lord and finding my way back to Him hearing a song by Mary Mary called, *Shackles*. I didn't typically listen to Christian music, but this song sounded different. The beat was obviously good, but it was the lyrics that seemed to penetrate my soul.

The more I listened to the song, the more I felt my convictions rise up. This was a double-edged sword for me. I felt the Lord calling me back to Him; however, I wasn't sure about giving up my miserable life that I had grown so comfortable with to live a life my heart was longing for.

I couldn't stop listening to this song. These words played over and over again:

"In the corners of my mind
I just can't seem to find a reason to believe
That I can break free
'Cause you see I have been down for so long
Feel like the hope is gone
But as I lift my hands, I understand

That I should praise you through my circumstance
Take the shackles off my feet so I can dance."

Boy, oh boy, it had been quite some time since I felt like putting on my dancing shoes. Yet this song seemed to shake loose everything I felt was holding me back in the cesspool of vomit I was living in. This song was my introduction to giving my life back to the Lord.

A few years later, after feeling a lot of conviction, I finally gave up the spiritual fight and decided to rededicate my life to the Lord. After doing so, He immediately began speaking to me about writing. Let me just inform you that I hated writing. It was extremely difficult for me to put on paper what I was thinking or what I was feeling on the inside. But, I followed His prompting and asked him what I should write about. He responded by telling me to write about all my past hurts, my mistakes, the demons I escaped from, the lessons I have learned, and how He turned my brokenness into being a triumphant warrior.

A few weeks into writing, I heard the Lord say, "One day you will be reading your own book." I thought to myself, What? I'm just journaling, Lord, not writing a book. He said, "No, I don't make mistakes, Lori. Hold on, my love, it's going to be a bumpy ride." I lay there in complete disbelief for what seemed like hours.

The next morning, after a long night of tossing and turning, I wondered how in the world He was going to make a writer out of me. I sat at church and heard the Lord say, "Shackles... this is the title for your book." The hair on my arms and the back of my neck stood straight up. I stood there stunned for a moment and then wrote the word "shackles" in my journal.

I felt the Lord had a larger-than-life task ahead of me and I knew I had to learn to trust Him completely so He could help me to fulfill it. And I am sure the Lord desires the same thing for you. However, there are common things that keep us from experiencing the freedom that God desires us to walk in. We will examine the things that have kept you shackled, and through my personal testimony show you how God can unleash Himself in your life.

In each chapter we will look at the pitfalls the Devil sets before us and how to overcome them. You will read about and learn the following:

- *Pinpoint defining moments that have affected your life and learn how to allow God to heal those broken places.*

- *How to say no to religion and yes to a personal relationship with God.*

- *How to turn your trials and tribulations into triumphant victories.*

- *How the most putrid of demonic spirits, including the spirit of death, cannot stand against God's plan for your life.*

- *How to turn over addiction, labels, and self-destructive behavior to God and allow him to take the fragmented pieces to create a beautiful masterpiece.*

- *How to uncover the hidden things in your life and allow the Lord to help you bring down the Goliaths in your life.*

- *How to discover who you are in the Lord and walk in your new identity.*

- *See how resting in the Lord will allow you to experience his peace and walk in your God-given callings.*

My prayer is that this book will help you learn the voice of God, listen to the voice of God, and move forward in what He has specifically designed for your life.

So, this is my prayer for you:

"Dear Heavenly Father, I come to you on behalf of every reader that opens the following pages, asking that you open their eyes and ears to hear your voice to see what you have in store for them. Move them in ways they have not yet experienced by showing them how very special they are. I pray that you allow the following words to penetrate their hearts to allow them to have a more intimate walk with you. I ask that the very words you have inspired me to write be used as a tool to awaken the spirit person inside of each reader and that you receive the Glory for it. I ask all this in the mighty name of Jesus, Amen."

CHAPTER 1
TO BE FOREVER CHANGED

———

FOR MOST OF US, there are circumstances that take place in life that are monumental in proportion. When these circumstances happen, they tend to shape who we are. I would like to share with you one of my moments.

When I was fourteen years old, a friend of mine from school, I'll call her Jodi, was having a party at her house and asked if I could come. Of course, I was thrilled because she was one of the popular kids at school and I knew the entire "cool crowd" would be there.

I don't know exactly how I talked my parents into letting me go because they were very strong Christians and were strict about letting us spend the night at places, but with their approval, I was packing my overnight bag. I was in complete disbelief that I had been invited to this party and tried to hurry out the door before my parents could change their minds.

I thought Jodi's mom was the coolest mom around because not only did she allow Jodi to have parties, but she also provided all of us kids with alcohol. I just knew her mom understood us because she treated us like grown-ups instead of children. With that being said, she immediately earned my undeserving respect.

Jodi was one of the kids in school whose parents didn't care what she did or whom she did it with. I was so jealous of her because she had so many friends, all the cool clothes, and the friendship of every popular kid in school. I'm sure her parents did this as a way of buying her affection.

They catered to her in all the wrong ways, but being a teenager, I wasn't into solving the problems of the world, I just wanted to have fun. I just felt fortunate that she included me as part of the gang.

The party started out in the garage, which had been decorated with Christmas lights and old junky furniture. Beside the worn-out furniture was a stereo system that was blaring all the popular hard rock '80s music. The Christmas lights were strung throughout the rafters and looked as if they were just thrown up in midair with no regard to how they landed.

The cigarette smoke was so thick, and the music was so loud you could hardly hear yourself think. The couches were lined up along the back wall of the garage. Sitting on the floor beside the couches were several coolers that were filled with beer and wine coolers. I couldn't believe it! Alcohol right there ready for us to drink! So that's what I did; I began to drink.

Kids were drifting in and out of the garage and soon the party spilled out onto the lawn. The music and laughter of teenagers was everywhere. Eventually, every corner of the yard had a group of kids in it as the yard seemed to be swallowed up by teenagers. Gossip about the latest boyfriend/girlfriend matches was being exchanged while everyone fixated on having fun. No one seemed to care about tomorrow, or the next hour, for that matter. We were doing what kids do—we were living in the moment.

I wanted to take mental pictures so as not to forget anything. It was like being in a movie while everything moved in slow motion. I felt like I was spinning in slow circles trying to take everything in. I wanted to remember what people were saying, what they wore, how I felt with this beer slowly intoxicating me. I wanted to remember every detail. I would not have to hear about the details from this party from my friends like all the previous times. This time I would have my own memories and stories of what started out to be one of the greatest nights of my life.

It only got better when the boy I had a crush on, "Elliot," walked in with his friends. I tried to make eye contact with him, but to no avail. He acted as if I was invisible. Feeling frustrated, I guzzled yet another drink so I could get the courage to go over and talk to him. I felt so nervous I just knew everyone could see my knees knocking as I started toward the garage.

Elliot and his friends found an available table and began playing a drinking game called quarters. I strolled over, pretending to have rock solid confidence but my quivering voice revealed something completely different. I looked straight at Elliot and asked if I could play. They all started laughing and goofing off. I tried to think of what I could say to save myself from this humiliation. At this point I wanted the room to suck me in.

I stood there trying to maintain my confidence, just waiting for someone to break the awkward silence. Someone finally spoke up and said I could play, but I only had one chance to bounce the quarter in. So, I grabbed the quarter, rolled my eyes and with my "whatever" attitude I flung the quarter down on the table. To my disbelief, my quarter found its way inside the glass. I snickered out loud like I knew what I was doing and secretly hoped that it would belittle the guys who had previously laughed at me. I told Elliot to take the shot. He looked at me and we locked eyes as he downed the drink I just gave him. I don't know if it was the alcohol or my adrenaline, but my heart began racing so fast and beating so loud it was a little difficult to breathe. He actually locked eyes with me. Did this mean he liked me? I was on Cloud Nine thinking life could not possibly get any better than this!

This drinking game went on for a while and I soon realized that every boy sitting at the table was making me do the drinks. I knew I was either going to puke or fall out of my chair. So before either incident occurred, I excused myself and slowly stumbled away. I felt completely out of control and was afraid I was going to fall down as I made my way out of the garage.

At this point it was getting dark outside, so I began looking around for my friends and my twin sister, Lisa. I realized just about everyone had moved the party inside the house.

I started walking toward the house, but I couldn't get there fast enough. It felt like it took me forever to walk only a few yards. My legs felt strange and weird, like there was a thousand pounds of lead in my shoes. I kept telling myself to just maintain focus on my friends through the window and keep walking. When I finally made my way up the porch steps and into the house, I saw food and beer cans everywhere! Empty potato chip bags had been thrown on the floor, candy wrappers spilled out of the kitchen trash can, a popcorn aroma came from the microwave, frozen pizzas were being cooked in the oven, and empty wine cooler bottles were on the kitchen counters. It looked like a bomb had gone off in there. But I did what everyone else was doing, I began to eat. This lasted until the food was gone.

Around midnight, the boys were told to leave. The co-ed part of the evening was coming to an end. So, all the girls stood on the porch and said good-bye to the boys we liked. Three of us girls received a kiss that night. There was no way life could ever get any better than this. I was exploding inside thinking; *He really does like me!* It's amazing how a pimply faced geeky boy could make me feel this alive!

Within an hour, all of us girls ended up on the living room floor in our pajamas watching scary movies and licking the crumbs out of the bottom of the last surviving potato chip bag. We were talking about how we all made a fool of ourselves laughing like typical fourteen-year-old girls as we reminisced about the evening. Every scenario had been replayed about four million times from every perspective...we just didn't want the night to end. We wanted to stay in the moment of having fun and being carefree. But one by one we were all being defeated by the alcohol and the late hour as we all began to pass out into a drunken, dead sleep.

A Real Live Boogeyman...

Sleeping like I had never slept before, I gradually came to or thought I was having a really bizarre dream. I was being picked up and carried through the house by my friend's eighteen-year-old brother, "Scott." What was happening to me? I was so out of it from being drunk that I blacked out. When I became coherent again, I opened my eyes to a dark blurry vision and felt myself being carried through the kitchen toward the basement door. I thought, *Why is he carrying me downstairs? There is nothing down there but...his bedroom!* I remember feeling so extremely tired and trying so hard to focus, but I just couldn't keep my eyes open, and I could not keep myself from blacking out again.

I woke up again to the smell of a cold musty basement. I was in a bed with Scott on top of me. The strong smell of cheap cologne mixed with sweat almost took my breath away. I was trying to look around and force myself to stay awake and to make sense of what was going on, but I couldn't find the strength to move. My body felt like it weighed a thousand pounds. As I tried to maneuver around, I tried to lift my head, but his fingers were intertwined in my hair, locking my head in place. A surge of panic rose up in me! This could not be happening!!!

I tried to look around to get my bearings but what I saw was shocking! I caught glimpses of myself, and I was naked! What in the world was going on? I was in complete disbelief as to what was happening. A flood of emotions and thoughts began racing through my mind. *It's not supposed to happen like this. This is so wrong.*

I knew I needed to totally wake up and become alert, but as I was trying to process exactly what was occurring, I was also at the same time trying to force my mind to shut down. It's like my mind was working but my body wasn't. I couldn't make it do anything. I was telling it to get up, to scream, to scratch, to maul, to completely pulverize him! I wanted to do something, anything to make this stop, but my body just wouldn't move! I felt like everything was moving in slow motion.

I realized that I couldn't move, I couldn't speak, and I couldn't breathe. All I could do was think *No!* My mind immediately began racing, thinking, *Get off of me! Stop! Don't do this to me. I'm just a kid! Why me? You're hurting me! Why won't my body move? I need to escape! Please someone help me! Get up, Lori! Get up! Get up and fight!*

I looked at that face intently—his sweat-beaded forehead. That disgusting smirk. His tousled coal black hair. His jet-black eyes that were torturing me. Looking at him all I could think was, I want to die! The intense hatred that suddenly washed over me was the most indescribable emotion I had ever had. It was like a consuming and overwhelming fire! I felt so completely out of control over what was happening to me. I felt paralyzed; paralyzed with fear, paralyzed with shame, and paralyzed from the alcohol.

At that moment, my body, my mind, and all of my emotions finally and completely shut down and went numb. I wasn't thinking of how to get away or how to survive this horrific experience. I wasn't feeling anything. And then it hit me: this was the feeling I was begging for, complete and utter "nothing." The tears streaming down the side of my face was the only thing that made me feel anything.

Realizing that even my most intense emotions were not making my paralyzed body move, I did the only thing I knew to do. I shut down and mentally drifted to a place I had never been before.

After he was finished, he got up and grabbed a towel, putting it around his waist. He threw my underwear and pajamas on the bed and walked away. He walked away like nothing had even happened.

How could he act like things were normal? Did he not realize what he had just done, or what he had taken from me? Was he going to run and hide and try and act like nothing had occurred? This reaction on his part scared me even more. What in the world was he thinking? He didn't even try to frighten me not to tell anyone. It's like I didn't matter enough for him to care what the outcome was. I was that worthless... I was that pathetic.

These were the thoughts that were running through my head as I was still trying to process what had just happened. I was in complete disbelief and shock over his actions and I knew that nothing would ever be the same again! I would never fully be me again.

The shame was already overwhelming me as I remembered not being able to physically move. My whole body was aching and throbbing and I smelled him everywhere–that sweaty-cheap cologne smell that made me want to throw up!

I laid there for what seemed like hours before I could conjure up enough will power and sobriety to get up and get out of there. As I stood up trying to wipe the tears from my eyes, it was then that I caught a glimpse of smeared blood on the sheets. For there in that bed he had not only stripped away my dignity and my trust in men, but he also stripped away my adolescence. He took away the one precious gift I could only give away to a man once, my virginity.

After grabbing my pajamas and putting them on, I stumbled up the stairs and ran to the bathroom, locking the door behind me knowing I was going to throw up. I collapsed to my knees in front of the toilet and began sobbing. After what seemed like hours of being there on the cold tile floor, I stood up and caught a glimpse of myself in the mirror. I saw the makeup-stained face staring back at me wondering, *where in the world did the little innocent girl disappear to?*

I wanted to shatter the mirror as I saw the hatred and disgust in my eyes. I cried uncontrollably wondering what to do next. I wanted to call my dad and have him come pick me up but I was too scared to call him. I turned on the sink and began splashing water on my face hoping it would wash away the disgust I felt, but the water did not have that kind of power. It just made me cold and I began to shiver as it trailed down my face, soaking my pajama top.

My mind was so unclear and I couldn't think of what to do next, so I unlocked the bathroom door and made my way back to the living room floor. I lay down, pulling the blankets over my head as if that would keep me safe. I began playing everything that had just happened over and over again in my mind as I cried throughout the night wondering how in the world I would ever survive this horrific experience.

At that point, I just wanted my daddy. I knew that if he was there he would save me and make things better. I wanted him to scoop me up in his arms and keep me safe, to erase everything that had just happened. I knew one embrace from my dad would somehow restore everything that had just been stripped away from me. But I just couldn't conjure up the courage to make that call.

THE BLACK HOLE!

I made the mistake of not telling my parents about that night and what had happened because of the shame that consumed me. Here I was, fourteen years old, and forced to deal with grown-up issues because everything normal in my life had just been ripped away in an instant. But on the other hand, I was still a little girl and wanted my daddy to make everything better. I knew once he wrapped his arms around me and I felt safe, it would somehow restore my faith in men, but I just couldn't tell my parents. I was afraid that my dad would spend the rest of his life in a place where I already was mentally, in prison!

So, I carried the guilt and secret around with me and forced myself to believe it was my fault because I had been drinking. How in the world could one decision to drink alcohol change my life forever? How could one mistake so quickly transform me into a person I could not recognize?

I never fully let in the fact that I was raped or understood that it wasn't my fault and I wasn't the one to blame until several years later. So I tried to forget about the whole incident and pretend like nothing had ever happened, but I soon realized that wasn't working.

As time passed, I just slipped further and further into a deep dark depression, a black hole that I would soon discover would be my home for the next twenty-plus years. I felt beyond worthless as I found myself just going through the motions of life because I still felt so numb inside.

After the rape, I got to the point where every little thing seemed to anger and enrage me until I was completely out of control. I would find myself punching holes in the walls just to express my anger. I would scream and yell at anyone who even dared to look my way. This behavior enabled me to release what I was feeling on the inside. I just wanted to hit, scream, and throw anything I could get my hands on. This was my way of purging my anger and regaining some control.

Every time the anger and hatred would rise up in me, my mind would shut itself down completely because it took me back to that one night when everything was out of my control. I couldn't stand the feeling of having no control. It made me extremely angry. But as time went on over the next several months, my mental state moved past numbing itself out. That's when I turned to alcohol and drugs on a regular basis for help. From the time the rape occurred, I drank constantly.

When I was high, I didn't have to feel or to think or to care about anything. I was able to numb out and close everything out. I wanted to remember nothing and feel nothing and the only way I knew how to do that was to stay high. I didn't care what happened to me because nothing could happen that would possibly compare to what I had just gone through.

Sometimes feeling angry and hateful was better than feeling nothing at all. I found myself doing just about anything and everything to hurt myself and others. Any self-destructive behavior I displayed was so enticing because I was hurting and dying on the inside and wanted something or someone to make it all disappear. And if it wasn't possible to make it disappear, I wanted to do whatever it took to make myself disappear!

So, I would go from fits of rage to getting drunk and stoned just to numb out. I soon found myself pushing the limits just a little bit further every time. I would drink more and more just to be able to black out. And if I didn't drink enough to get to that point, I would put something with it like smoking pot, popping pills, or dropping acid. I found myself doing anything to get myself to pass out. But after a while, it took more and more alcohol and drugs to give me the results I was looking for. Before long I found myself getting high on a daily basis.

I felt as if I was damaged goods. I kept wondering why this had happened to me. I couldn't get over the rape and now I wanted revenge! I wanted him dead and tortured. I often sat around thinking of ways to torment and humiliate him. I wanted him to feel the same way I felt that night. These thoughts somehow made me feel better even if they were only in my mind.

Instead of trying to heal what I was suffering through, I only concentrated on the hatred and disgust I felt for him. He soon consumed my every thought. I was obsessed. If I was tired, I blamed him because I would be coming down off of a high trying to forget what he had done to me. If I was sad, I blamed him because he was the one who had put me in this prison. If I was distrusting of men, it was his fault for ripping that trust away from me.

I soon allowed this man to control every aspect of my life by dictating what my future would be, because I was too ashamed to fully face what had happened and to take full control back for fear of losing that control again. Before long I took no responsibility for my life and my actions. It was much easier to blame him and play the role of victim. Being a victim soon became my *entire* identity.

I could not understand how another human being could be so cruel, thoughtless, and self-serving. I hated this man with everything in me, which made me feel even more lost and alone. This dark pit I lived in was the deepest, darkest, and most repulsive place I had ever been and I could not escape it. It was turning me into a person I didn't recognize, a person I didn't like, and a person that was unworthy of anything but heartache.

With that one act, this man had made me crawl inside myself, hating the world, trusting virtually no one, and losing pieces of myself that were not to be found again for more than twenty years!

This incident allowed the enemy to wreak havoc on me with guilt and shame that tormented me from the time I was 14 until I was about 34. I learned to abuse myself using alcohol and adopted the victim mentality behavior because it fed the very monster inside of me. While feeding the "shame" spirit and the "guilt" spirit, it soon began shaping how I viewed myself, which pushed me further inside that black hole. What became scary in such a short timeframe was that black hole began to feel very comfortable and like home to me.

WAITING TO FORGIVE...

I thought this incident had changed my life forever because it was where everything stemmed from. It is what changed me into the person

I hated and eventually tried to torture every day in one way or another. I felt like I was worthy of nothing and that I deserved heartache. I felt like I wasn't good enough for anyone to treat me with any type of respect, but at the same time, I constantly walked around with a chip on my shoulder wanting someone to ask me to lose it so I could explode with anger.

I looked for ways to provoke arguments because it allowed me to express what I was feeling inside. I felt like it was eating me alive and if I couldn't get it out in the open, it would consume me completely and I would be lost forever!

If I could sum up with one sentence how I felt for most of my life (pre-Jesus days), it would be this: *I felt like the world owed me something, but I didn't feel worthy enough to receive it.* I lived in this pitiful cycle as it repeated itself over and over again.

Anyone who tried to reach out to me was ripped to shreds, but people who steered clear of me only tortured me more because they were doing the very thing I wanted to do to myself but couldn't: escaping me!

At times I missed the old me so much and I had forgotten what it felt like to just be a kid. I wanted to feel the innocence and longed to be "normal" again.

I had buried those feelings for so long I didn't even realize I had not dealt with them. I got so used to pushing everything down, thinking there was no way to ever heal on my own. It was like a runaway train destroying everything in its path. It eventually jumps the track completely leaving so much destruction along the way.

Do I, or Don't I?

What helped me heal from this horrific event was remembering the story of Jesus' crucifixion. I began viewing it differently than when I had heard the story as a kid. I thought of what Jesus went through as He gave His life for us on the cross–the humiliation He suffered as He was mocked and de-robed, naked from the waist down as He was paraded around. He was tortured with the skin being ripped away from His body, His facial hair literally pulled out, spit on and beaten beyond human recognition, finally to be hung on a cross to eventually die for our sins. He didn't have the ability to stop the abuse from occurring and this allowed me to have a revelation moment that Christ was a safe place because he truly understood my past pain. It's a story that millions of people over a few thousand years have heard...but does it really hit home for you?

To be honest, it didn't for me until the Lord started His work on me and my healing process. After the Lord removed a few layers from me, my thought process, which had been, *with one horrific act this man made me crawl inside myself hating the world, trusting virtually no one and losing pieces of myself, shifted to, with that one loving act, this man named Jesus enabled me to find myself, trusting entirely in him, and finding all the broken pieces to make myself whole again; he is changing me forever!*

Talk about powerful! It touched me so deeply that His love for me meant more than anything the Devil could do to me. The Lord was showing me firsthand about his perfect love!

The Bible says in Luke 23:34, "Father forgive them for they know not what they do." Jesus took this on and endured it all for us so that we might have enough compassion to forgive people who do wrong to us. The Bible says it's easy to forgive your brother, but it's a sacrifice to forgive your enemy, to pray for your enemies so that they may see the glory of God.

I'm going to be completely honest: reading it in the Bible is so much easier than putting it into action. It was extremely difficult to pray for "Scott." I didn't feel that he deserved to be forgiven.

But if Jesus can ask for forgiveness toward the people that hung Him on the cross while taking in his last breath of air, then I can forgive the man who wronged me and what he did to me. So that's what I did. I prayed, and prayed, and prayed some more to try and find forgiveness in my heart. After a while, I thought I *might possibly* want to try and forgive him, but I still couldn't find it within myself to do so. Did I want to forgive him or didn't I?

With no change in my heart toward him, the Lord showed me how to change my prayer by asking Him to *give me the desire* deep in my heart to really *want* to forgive this man. I didn't want to forgive him just because it's the good Christian thing to do. I wanted to try and really let go, release every emotional struggle I had associated with him and the rape. Guess what? God granted me that desire.

I'm not going to lie and say it was instantaneous, because it wasn't. But the Lord showed me how to align my prayers with His will, and that is when I saw changes in myself and my mindset.

I started looking back at yearbook pictures trying to humanize him and rid my disgusting memory of that face I had etched in my mind several years ago. Those jet-black eyes I had seen in my memory for twenty years started to soften just a little. Instead of seeing a monster, I began to see a young man who was being used by the enemy.

Over time, every disgusting detail about him started to change. It did not come easy at first. Lord knows the struggles I had with this hurdle, but over time God replaced all the grudges and un-forgiveness I had with compassion. This was the beginning of the Lord revealing to me what it meant to have true joy.

Nothing ever happened to Scott. I didn't go to the authorities. I didn't tell his parents. I kept everything inside and isolated myself. Once I was ready to face the music and deal with the situation with a sober mind and allow God to show me how to release my feelings about it, twenty years had passed.

To my regret, I didn't tell my parents about the rape until I was almost done writing this book. I kept it from them because I didn't want them to unnecessarily hurt from the situation. Looking back over my life, I wish I would have shared it with them sooner and given them the opportunity to help me through it.

After I told them what happened, of course it was painful to hear something like that about your child, but I think they both see that the Lord is using my hurts to help other people. I think they see their prayers for me over the years are finally coming into fruition and witnessing firsthand how God can truly give beauty for ashes. The Bible says in Isaiah 61:3, "And provide for those who grieve in Zion— to bestow on them a crown of beauty instead of ashes, the oil of joy instead of mourning, and a garment of praise instead of a spirit of despair." This is a perfect example of Gods restoration process.

I pray often that guilt has not dictated and guided Scott's life and that God shows him the same forgiveness and mercy that He has shown me.

PEELING AN ONION...

It's "Godronic." Yes, this is my word and you will hear me say it quite often. It is something ironic that in true essence is really a God thing. My goal is to have that in the *Webster's Dictionary* one day! But it is Godronic thinking back at that incident of how I wanted nothing more than my daddy's arms wrapped around me because he always made me feel safe. I trusted him to take care of whatever it was I asked of him.

I am extremely privileged to have a dad who emulates our Heavenly Father so well. His entire being exudes the Spirit of God and when you come into his presence, you just know that there is something special about him. He truly loves with Gods love. If you ever get the privilege to meet him, you will understand the second you lay eyes on him. He never judges. He never speaks an ill word about anyone. I can count on one hand how many times I have seen him angry. Even when I thought he should have washed his hands of me and sent me away to a rehab facility or a place that would try and "knock some sense into my head," he never showed disappointment in me as a person, my actions, yes, but not me personally. He always made sure I knew I was loved and I was a prize. He disciplined with his "look." He would try and hide his shattered eyes when he would encounter my latest shenanigans, but it was his look that was enough to drop me to my knees. He didn't have to whip me, or ground me, or take my car privileges away....it was just "daddy's look."

And the Lord wants this same relationship with us. He wants to give you that peace of mind that there is nothing you can do to take away His love. He wants us to know that He will give us beauty for ashes. Look a little deeper at that phrase, "beauty for ashes."

Everyone wants to stick that label on as a "God sticker" per se. But what it really says is that you *came out* of a horrific experience and God is going to do something amazing with it. That's the key; you didn't die in your situation. You may have felt like dying, but God brought you out.

He never promised that our lives would be easy or without trials and tribulations, but He did promise that He would never leave us or forsake us. He promised to give us the knowledge and wisdom to face whatever situation arises if we seek Him first. God will always provide you with the armor you need for whatever battles you are embarking on. Ephesians 6:11 says, "Put on the full armor of God so that you can take your stand against the Devil's schemes." But the key to that is *putting it on.* The armor won't do you any good just sitting there in your closet.

But what does it mean to "put on the armor of God?" It means choosing to walk in salvation. Choosing to walk in truth. Choosing to walk in faith. All while using the Spirit of God to direct you on *how* to use them. Because let's face it, we are not strong enough, wise enough, durable enough to live our lives in our own strength for any length of time.

Oh you can muddle through life, but it is not walking in the complete fullness of how God wants us to live if we are not using His free gifts He has given us.

If you choose to *put on* truth and *use* it, then the spirit of truth is fighting for you and combatting every demon in Hell that is rising up against the spirit of truth. *Using* truth helps you guard your tongue. It is shaping the way you think, about others and about yourself. The armor of truth is combatting every wicked lie that comes against you.

If you choose to *put on* and *use* the helmet of salvation, then the enemy can't penetrate your mind. It's like hearing a coworker spread lies about you regarding something that isn't true, like stealing. It attacks your character. When you choose to *"put on"* the armor, those lies come to you but are soon thrown off with the Spirit inside of you telling you, "do not entertain those lies, listen to me *only*...you are not who the enemy says you are. Remember, you are fearfully and wonderfully made. You are the apple of my eye. Put me in charge of this situation and see what I will do with it. Rest in the fact that I am a good and just Father." Do you see where I am going with this?

Let's remember to put on the *full* armor. Because let's face it, the helmet of salvation probably works best when working in tandem with the belt of truth, the shield of faith, and the sword of the Spirit. You see, if a person were to just put on the belt of truth, he would not be allowing God to use the shield or sword to help in this war we are in. I mean who wants to go to war and fight a battle without protection that is freely given? I don't believe anyone would opt for that situation.

Putting on the full armor works best when you choose to use them *all* because that is when we are *fully* guarded. And who doesn't want to be fully guarded against the schemes of the enemy?

I had gotten to the point where I was tired of feeling angry and empty inside. I believe the Lord allowed me to get to the place that nothing I did soothed those "God holes" anymore. That's when the Lord started planting seeds within me over the years of how to forgive. You may be saying the same thing and remembering things the Lord has said to you in the past. Things He is reminding you of. Don't find it strange if right this minute you feel a stirring in your spirit of past dreams and visions he has given you because He is ready to breathe life into them right now.

Fortunately, through a lot of praying, and I mean *a lot* of prayers, I have, through the grace of God, completely forgiven the man who raped me. I know it sounds so simple and easy because you are reading a few sentences that state the fact of my forgiveness. But it was a long and *difficult* process. The length of the process was because of my unwillingness to trust God in the situation for quite some time. But once I gave it over to the Lord, He began showing me I was guarding my demons with my victim mentality. Once He brought that to my attention and what an ugly thing it truly was, I finally allowed Him to begin stripping it away. I wanted the Lord to heal those deep dark places that only He knew about. He guided me to trust Him enough to open up the most desolate places of my soul to him and trust that what he was going to do with it was going to be magnificent.

When He whispered to me that it's time to let it all go, I had to choose to trust Him, and believe me when I say it did not come easily. This was me *taking up* my shield of faith that I could trust Him. This is the only piece of armor that we don't wear as a regular part of our uniform-we take it up during battle, but it is such an important piece to the puzzle. The Bible says in Hebrew 11:6 that without faith, it is impossible to please Him.

The Lord guided me to trust him and held my hand through the entire process. He was the one that removed the spirit of victim mentality from me once I allowed him to. Once that was removed, He started working on all of the other areas that desperately needed His touch.

It was like peeling an onion, layer on top of layer, with tear-filled eyes. When the Lord guided me to release the "hatred" layer, He showed me unconditional love. When He peeled away the "hurt" layer, He gave me comfort. The layer of "unworthiness" was replaced with self-respect. The layer of "unforgiveness" was replaced with deep compassion for people.

Once I chose to give this over to Him, He showed me that I no longer had to carry that burden anymore and I didn't have to hate anymore. Hating takes so much energy, not to mention how time consuming it is, especially if you do it well–and that was one thing I did extremely well. If you really hate someone, your every thought is focused on that person.

I no longer have to just exist and suffer through each day. I now can rejoice that God has brought me through what appeared to be the darkest time in my life and a circumstance that appeared to have shaped my entire life.

I am now a mighty woman of God who is strong and powerful because I am choosing to listen to the Lord's voice and what He has to say about me; how he values me, and what I mean in the Kingdom of God. I realize more and more that God can heal anyone who is a willing vessel. God tells me in one way or another every day, "Lori, my darling, *you are worth it!*" And you, My Friend, are worth it, too.

God wants to show you how He can change your mindset regarding the situation that has tried to define you. The reason you are reading this book right now is because God is saying, *It's time. It's time to let it go and start the healing process.* It may not be easy, but I can promise you it will be worth it.

If you feel the sting in your eyes right now from the tears welling up because you feel in your heart that it's time to let go of your past hurts, then My Dear, let's take that journey together.

If you feel the anger rising up, then let's get you to the point of uncovering the wound. Because anger is the coating that covers up hurt.

Do *not* allow the enemy to have the next several chapters of your very own story. With the help of the Holy Spirit, you can write what you want! You don't have to be in bondage to the stupid Devil any longer! It's your time to author your story.

If you want to be free from anger, write it. If you want to forgive the person that wronged you, write it. If you no longer want to be a slave to your past mistakes, write it. If you want complete freedom, write it. Whatever it is that has you in bondage, you have the power to write it.

God is giving you the key to make your story absolutely beautiful. What will you write?

As you think about this and how you want your story to change, remember this: God's mercy and restoration are waiting for you. So don't put Him in a box and think small, puny changes. Think *big!* Think *complete restoration!* Think *complete joy!* He's the creator of the entire universe. You can trust that He can handle your situation and help make it the most beautifully written story you have ever heard.

I trust that God is stirring something up in your spirit right now that has you ready to take hold of the changes that He wants to make in your life. When your mindset starts to shift, there is no stopping you. When there is a willing vessel, God can do anything.

Are you ready? I believe you are. Hold on tight, My Friend, you are about to embark upon a journey that is going to blow your mind!

~ One link has been broken ~

CHAPTER 2
THE TURNING POINT

I SHARED WITH YOU the incident that happened when I was fourteen years old, but now I would like to backtrack a little bit to show you what led up to the event.

When I was a little girl around the age of five, my parents would put us on the church bus to attend church. My sisters and I couldn't wait for Sundays to roll around. We knew as soon as we saw the church bus pull up, we were in for a treat. The church bus provided us with free snacks, which usually consisted of a hotdog, a bag of chips, or a piece of that rock-hard pink bubblegum that only stayed soft long enough to blow bubbles for about three minutes. Growing up poor, this was a huge treat for us.

As the driver picked us up, he would mark our attendance card. Once we reached twelve Sundays in a row we received a free miniature Bible, the kind that you could fit in your coat pocket.

I remember the weekend of our twelfth Sunday. My parents wanted to go out of town and we would have to miss church. This meant we wouldn't receive our free Bible and we would have to start the process all over again. We threw a fit until my parents relented and allowed us to attend church that Sunday.

We got off of that bus like we owned the world. Our bellies were full and there in our hands was our brand-spanking new Bibles.

This took place before the Lord got a hold of my parents and they made him the Lord of their lives. But from the moment my parents became Christians, church became a huge part of my life growing up.

My parents never gave us an option of whether we would attend church or not. You just went like clockwork every Sunday morning, every Sunday night, and every Wednesday night. Those boundaries were set and never questioned.

When I was nine years old, my family and I attended a church that ran like clockwork. The services opened with a prayer, followed by singing a few songs. We moved into the testimonial portion of the service, the church received tithes, and then the pastor preached.

He would preach on how to get saved by confessing your sins. You would then ask God to be the Lord of your life and confess that Jesus died on the cross to give you eternal life. You were then officially saved. That was "religion" in a nutshell. The services were pretty straightforward and extremely repetitive with the only thing changing from service to service were the songs we sang, like *"The Old Rugged Cross"* or *"I'll Fly Away."* There was no room for the Lord's Spirit to move around. It was as if the order of service was more important than the Spirit of God.

It was renowned for telling you how to get saved, but that's it. They didn't explain what to do next. So I did what I knew to do: I repented and accepted the Lord as my Savior. I knew that if I followed all Ten Commandments, got baptized, and went to church every Sunday that I was saved. I followed the protocol like everyone else. But I couldn't help but feel like I was missing something. I thought, *I just go to church and that's it—that's all I have to do?*

I felt this tugging sensation deep inside my soul speaking to me, but I couldn't quite make out what it was, and being a kid, I had no clue what it meant.

Now what do I do? How do I walk the right way as a Christian? How do I have a personal relationship with God? How do I make all those stories of the Bible somehow mean something to me? "How do

I?" was a question I had, but I didn't have the first clue how to obtain the answers I was searching for.

I figured everyone was experiencing what I was going through so I thought it was normal. Strange, yes. But normal. I also feared that the elders of the church would think I was "just a kid" and had no real clue as to what I really wanted out of a genuine Christian relationship with God. But I did; I just didn't know the first thing about maintaining my "Christian status" as I wanted it to be.

So I did what I knew to do. I would leave church on Sunday night and would go about my everyday life. I obviously would sin again or do something wrong, and *boom*, I was guilt-ridden. I was running back down to the altar and repenting for the hundredth time the very next church service getting "saved" again. I felt horrible knowing that I had done something wrong and I had to wait until the next time I went to church to make my way down to the altar to repent and get re-saved. This ritual of mine went on for a very long time.

Magical Altar?

I never spoke to anyone about the way I was feeling so I walked around constantly confused about religion. I would be so confused when I would feel something on the inside that I didn't see displayed in our church. I thought I was the only one to feel this way because I never heard anyone say he or she had the same confusion I had.

I didn't know I could have my own personal relationship with God and talk to Him any time I wanted to. I was under the impression that it had to be done in church, at the altar, and only at altar call. I honestly thought for the longest time that there was some magical power in the altar itself and that was the reason we prayed there for forgiveness.

I never realized the heavy burdens I carried around as a young Christian. I often wondered how I could make the whole process a little easier and become something more fulfilling. At this point, I was carrying around more burdens as a Christian than I would have ever carried around as a pre-believer.

I felt that if you had participated in the weekly rituals of the church service then you were doing everything you needed to do to maintain your good standing with God. Somehow, I just knew God wanted more from me and for me–I just couldn't quite figure out what I needed to get or how to get it. But, I so longed for something deeper and more spiritual.

It was a frustrating feeling knowing I had to find something but I had no clue where to look, what it was, what it looked like, or what it felt like. I just knew it existed and I was determined to find it. I was so desperate for something God had placed in me at some point in time; I had just not figured it out entirely.

God had let me in on a little secret but I didn't know the combination to open it completely. He was telling me that I was right and to keep pressing forward, that there was something more and that I had to seek whole-heartedly. So, I hung on in search of the "God relationship" with every shred of faith I had so I could find what it was I was looking for.

Through all my searching and feeling like I needed a small breakthrough of some sort, God sent my favorite singing group, The Abundant Life, to lead worship at our Church one night. I felt more alive inside when they would visit our church and an overwhelming sense of peace, almost as if this was part of the combination to unlock the secret.

One of my favorite memories was the night the Lord's presence fell in that place. Being a thirteen year old girl it was uncool to be excited about a "Christian singing group", but I didn't care, the place was electric when they started singing.

When the music started, I immediately felt goosebumps pop all over me and the hair on the back of my neck stood straight up. I just knew I couldn't remain in my seat any longer so I quickly made my way to the altar in hopes of getting closer to whatever it was I was experiencing. The closer I got, the more I felt His presence. I felt shaky, lightheaded, and an overwhelming urge to cry. I knelt down at the altar and just let myself go. I sat there sobbing with my face in my hands. I had an overpowering sensation of shame and unworthiness like I wasn't good enough to be in His presence, but at the same time felt so greedy wanting more because there was complete and utter peace surrounding me. I never wanted this feeling to end. I felt so loved that I could almost feel His arms wrapped around me. I felt like He entered that room and walked over to me, grabbed my hand, and just loved on me.

At this point I knew I wanted this "God relationship" and was thrilled to know that He really did exist. This was the God presence I had so longed for. I didn't just want to read about history stories from the Bible. I wanted my own God story, and I had just encountered one! I knew deep in my soul that God was in the church that night and He was looking for anyone who would invite Him in. I not only wanted to invite Him in, I wanted Him to never leave. I didn't want to live another moment not feeling the Spirit of God wrapped all around me. I desperately wanted this feeling to last forever.

After several minutes at the altar I got up and moved back to my seat. I would be lying if I said I wasn't fearful of never experiencing the Lord like that again. Through all of my searching, He unlocked the combination for me; I had just had my first real experience with the Spirit of God.

I felt like I could not breathe without breathing Him in. God was everywhere; It was by far the most bizarre but the most desired sensation I had ever experienced. I wanted to bottle this feeling and take it with me because I could not fathom the idea of never feeling it again. I wanted to be able to dab a little bit here, dab a little bit there, like an expensive bottle of perfume. But I knew I would not be able to contain myself the way I felt. I would have poured the entire bottle over my head the first chance I got!

I couldn't believe God had found me worthy enough to give me such a wonderful gift of my very own. This left me on a spiritual high and craving more of God that I could not quench. I didn't want to live on the scraps from the week before; I wanted a new encounter with Him. I wanted to be in His presence from the moment I woke up in the morning until I fell asleep at night. But I didn't know at that time how to make this happen. I was still thinking I had to be in church praying at the altar to have an encounter with Him.

Unfortunately, those few church services a year were just enough to get you hungry and wanting more! By the next church service things were back to their normal repetitive "schedule" again. It left me praying for the Spirit of God to come and consume the church leaders so that when God did show up they would allow Him to be there! It was like winning the lottery and no one turning in the winning ticket.

My church life continued with no excitement, no fire, and no zeal. I wanted God so desperately—not a religion or church—but God! But I didn't know how to get that relationship on my own. I soon realized I would have to wait another year for a "special service" before having another God experience like I had just had. Waiting to feel His presence again was like waiting a year to eat. I just knew I would shrivel up and spiritually die.

After a while it became more and more difficult to find the motivation to go to church looking for God and never finding Him. I was getting used to the all-too-familiar feeling of emptiness that the church services provided, so I started to give up knowing that those few times a year were not enough to get me through the temptations and peer pressure I was struggling with on a day-to-day basis. It was easier to give up and have no expectations at all than to have unmet expectations.

Unfortunately, the peer pressure was becoming much easier to submit to because I was no longer feeling the need to explain my relationship with God to anyone. To be completely honest, my relationship with Him became something of the past, the slow fade away from Him took place before I even realized it had happened.

Within a few short years I became extremely rebellious and started acting out in ways that were not the "normal" me. It got to the point that my parents literally had to force me to go to church. It was odd; I actually detested going to church and everything it stood for.

I knew I could not live in the ways of the world and be a Christian and I had to decide which lifestyle I was going to live. James 3:11-12 says, "Can both fresh water and salt water flow from the same spring? My Brothers, can a fig tree bear olives, or a grapevine bear figs? Neither can a salt spring produce fresh water? Neither can a salt spring produce fresh water."

I didn't even know this scripture existed at the time, but I knew it in my heart. I couldn't go to church every Sunday and live like the Devil the other six days a week. I was more tormented living on both sides of the fence knowing I had to pick a side because that fence post had poked me long and hard enough.

So, I chose. I felt at this point it was easiest to go with the ways of the world and not have any expectations put on me, so that's what I slowly did. I mentally drifted away from the church and the longing for a personal relationship with God and let Satan take over.

I began hanging out with the "wrong" crowd and doing things I shouldn't be doing.

Let me just say that the enemy is a liar. He played with my mind, telling me that I didn't want the Christian label anymore and that I wanted to be free from it all. He dangled freedom in front of my face, but instead it was a suffocating prison.

Tea Sipping Angels...

In sharing this with you I want you to take a strong, hard, close look at your situation right now. Do you attend a church? A small group or a mentor/discipleship program? Are your spiritual needs being met? Meaning, do you leave church feeling more frustrated and wounded than when you entered the building? Do you feel the presence of God when you are at church? Or for that matter, do you feel His presence at all? Are your children fighting you about not wanting to go to church?

My prayer for you is that you realize your children are not too young to have a personal relationship with the Lord. Children are looking for guidance and encouragement from the adults in their lives to help set the foundation for a personal relationship with Him.

God will take the very heart of a child and turn the world upside down with it, because that child believes whole-heartedly that He will show up and deliver what He promised! We are to have childlike faith, to believe without seeing. The Bible says in Matthew 18:3, "And he said: 'Truly I tell you, unless you change and become like little children, you will never enter the kingdom of Heaven.'"

Be aware of falling into the trap of being comfortable. Do not exclude a relationship with God because you're comfortable, or because you have always gone to a particular church, or because your friends go there. Because if God is not there and you do not have a personal relationship with Him, you are missing out on the most awesome journey you will ever take!

I guarantee once you have had an encounter with Him, it will change your life forever! You will find yourself craving not just the experience, but God Himself, who gives those experiences. You won't go to church out of obligation but out of a true desire in your heart. You will find yourself doing anything to keep that close and intimate relationship with him.

I think about what would have happened to me if I had gone to a church that actually had God in it on a regular basis. I bet you I would have figured out a way to bottle God by now! Seriously, I am not here to bash churches. I honestly have to say that sometimes I receive more from God and hear His voice more when I am in my own prayer closet. I have the most breakthrough moments with Him when I am behind closed doors with my Christian music playing and I am seeking to be in His presence. I know that He will show up because I am seeking Him with my whole heart, and not out of obligation. The Bible says that in Jeremiah 29:13: "You will seek me and find me when you seek me with all your heart."

But unfortunately, a religious attitude will keep people feeling that if they attend church, tithe, and say "Amen" a few times that they are fulfilling an obligation as a Christian. But God doesn't want a sense of obligation, He wants you.

We can either pray dead meaningless words out of obligation because of some outrageous checklist we have created in our own mind of what a good Christian should do, or we can pray as if our very life depends on it! Or the salvation of your children depends on it! Or the doctor's report you are waiting for depends on it! Get that fire in your belly and pray *big bodacious* prayers, my friends! It is life changing and lifesaving!

Your prayers will absolutely change the atmosphere in the spiritual realm! Dispatch those fighting angels on your behalf. And why not? God has assigned you your very own angels. It's not just Charlie's Angels; it's better! It's Toni's Angels, Tammy's Angels, Michele's Angels, Micky's Angels, and Sienna's Angels! They are there waiting for the words to come out of your mouth so they know what to do. Are your words going to be bold and powerful and give them something to do today–something to fight for? Or are you going to have a dead prayer life and leave your angels sitting on the sidelines sipping sweet tea with nothing to do?

I know I want more than anything to have God fighting for me and to have the atmosphere change because what I contain is life changing. Once you realize that sweetheart, watch out Devil! No more will we be victims of a lifeless, nonexistent prayer life!

I am not going to lie and say that my prayer life started out beautifully with eloquently spoken words. I didn't feel my words were good enough to actually speak to the Creator of the Universe, the Alpha and Omega, The Beginning and the End. God. But I did start, which at first felt very strange. I'm speaking into the atmosphere to an invisible God...I felt like an idiot. But I continued beyond what my carnal mind was trying to tell me.

So I began researching Bible scriptures that would help me understand the whole praying process. Ask and you shall receive, check! Whatever you ask in my name without doubting shall be yours, blah blah blah, yeah, I got that, too. The prayers of the righteous man availeth much, yep, check. So, let me get this straight. You pray, wait for God to deliver, and voilà...God: my personal genie in a bottle. I mean, come on people, this religion thing isn't that hard!

Until you ask for something God didn't intend for you to have. That's when the foundation of who you are and what you believe starts rocking a little. You do what you know to do. You pray and ask God for whatever it is you want and wait for Him to deliver it to you on His white horse and blowing trumpets, right? Not hardly, My Friend.

Things look so easy in all the Bible stories because the story has already been written and the ending has already been seen. I found myself reading these stories asking why in the world these people didn't see that their faith and prayers were working because the end of the story showed God to have worked out the entire situation perfectly. So I asked the Lord, "Why can't my situation work out so beautifully?" and He responded by telling me, "The people in the stories you are referencing had complete trust and faith in Me that I would answer their prayers. They cast all their cares upon me. You cast your cares upon me to only pick them up again not trusting entirely and not having enough faith that I, too, will answer your prayers. Get out of the boat, Lori, and completely trust in me." Just like the story of when Jesus called Peter out of the boat in Matthew 14, the Lord called me out of my small confining boat!

However, thinking something in your head and actually doing it are two different things. And boy did that lesson take a long time for me to really comprehend. If my prayers weren't answered, which most of the time they weren't, I questioned God about why He hadn't answered them. I don't like to admit that God and I went a few rounds before I saw things with spiritual eyes and began to truly trust him.

GENIE IN A BOTTLE...

I'm going to be completely transparent here and tell you I was a little spoiled in my thinking and wanted God to be my genie in a bottle. I had a hard time seeing into the spiritual realm and seeing God work on my behalf. I felt that if things didn't work out exactly how I wanted them to that He wasn't answering my prayers. Wrong.

He couldn't answer my prayers the way I wanted because He had to work on me first. I was praying selfish prayers that were not furthering the Kingdom of God, they were only furthering me.

The harder I prayed for God to change that annoying person in my life, the more annoying the person became. The situation just seemed to escalate. But why didn't the situation change?

I'll share with you a little secret. It's because my prayers were self-serving, and I had a prideful spirit. A prideful person does *not* want to admit he or she is prideful, well, because we are prideful. It's kind of funny actually; the enemy has us chasing our own tail on this one. Oh my goodness, this was not a fun lesson to learn. The harder I prayed the more God put the squeeze on me.

This went on until God revealed to me that my heart wasn't right. When I asked God to show me how to trust Him fully in my situation, that's when I started seeing consistent breakthroughs in my prayer life. Oh, there are still storms that I face and my faith shakes a little bit.

I'm sure you can relate to this. But praying from a heart the Lord reconstructed is where you will see results. He taught me that the storms in life are to show a person what he or she is really made of. A person learns more about themselves and their faith going through the storms than at any other time in life.

When we learn to pray for God's will in a situation so that the Kingdom of Heaven is advancing instead of us, *that* is when we will see our prayers being answered. Having the mind of Christ helps our prayers to penetrate the very atmosphere.

So, as I continue to share my story with you and we journey on what promises to be a rough but hopeful road, I realized that God was there with me the entire time, even when I didn't see it, just like He is there with you. Every step I took and every crossroad I came to was my individual road map that led me to where I am today.

I am able with His grace to look at where He has brought me from and thank Him for the lessons I've learned along the way. And I promise you will do the same.

~ Another link has been broken ~

CHAPTER 3
LOSS AND LIFE

AFTER LIVING IN AN EMOTIONAL PIT of depression for several months after the rape, the fear of someone figuring out my secret was almost unbearable. The thought of having to tell anyone was unfathomable after working so hard to bury myself deep inside this exceptionally small box that had become my identity. I wanted more than anything to try and tear down the walls I had built, but I didn't know how.

As I tried to climb my way over that wall, I started to regain a sense of my old self. I began hanging out with my friends and playing sports again. For the first time in a really long time I felt like I wanted to move on and try and find a little bit of peace and happiness. With that, along came a boy–I'll call him Alexander–who I ended up dating for four years during high school. We started hanging out and passing notes to each other in class and smile at each other as we passed in the hallway between classes. The innocence between us I felt was refreshing. This is how things should be. I couldn't believe I had butterflies in my stomach over a boy.

I felt such relief that it was possible not to go the rest of my life feeling a hatred and mistrust for men. It was as if I could see a little piece of hatred being chipped away and flung into the air far away from me.

Alexander was on the football team and I was on the tennis team so we were able to see each other after school every day. This soon turned into spending all of our free time together in the evenings, as well. We were pretty much becoming inseparable. After dating for about six months, I just knew in my teenage mind that this was love. He had earned enough of my trust to make our relationship feel as solid as I knew how to feel at that time.

After a little time passed he wanted to take things to the next level. Kissing wasn't satisfying him anymore. To be honest, I was feeling the same way. He swore his undying love to me and that it would only confirm our commitment to each other. In my mind, I couldn't bear the thought of telling him I wasn't a virgin anymore and what had happened to me. I was so afraid he would think less of me and wouldn't want me anymore because I was "used." Uncovering this secret to him was absolutely paralyzing me.

I was able to sidestep the conversation for a while when it would come up, but not for long. He started getting more and more impatient and couldn't understand why I loved him but wouldn't give myself to him physically.

After much preparation for his departure once he knew my secret about the rape, I told him. I told him how disgusted I felt about myself, how I felt like I wasn't a whole person anymore, how I had been stripped of my dignity and self-worth. I had absolutely no self-respect left at this point. But to my amazement he still wanted me. I couldn't believe it. He actually became extremely infuriated on my behalf when I told him my secret.

I had never seen this side of him before, the things that came spewing from his mouth and what he was going to do to this guy were so shocking to me. I honestly thought he was going to kill him. Well, this only confirmed my feelings for him and that I could trust him. I knew he cared for me deeply enough to be enraged on my behalf. He was a man I could trust with my most sacred secrets and love me in spite of them. Yes, he was turning into the prince charming I had longed for.

I soon realized that my entire life was starting to revolve around him. I wanted to hold on to him with everything in me because I just knew that no one else in his right mind would ever want me now. Especially because I was sneaking out of my house every night to be with him. Sex with my boyfriend began to erase the filthiness I had felt about sex before. I started associating sex with love and security, not rape.

It wasn't long before we were going to our friend's house every night to get high, which lasted until four or five o'clock in the morning. If we lost track of time and I was running late to make it home before my parents woke up, I would walk back to my house while it was still dark outside. I'd be so high I would have to follow the yellow lines in the middle of the road to keep me on the right road home.

When I got out of school I would barely make it to my bedroom before passing out from exhaustion. This hard life of partying until all hours of the night went on until I was so tired all the time I didn't have enough energy to do anything properly. I became very distracted and moody with everyone. But I continued to live this lifestyle because it was soothing to me to be able to control what I did and when I did it. If I wanted to party with my friends and play "house" with my boyfriend, it was entirely up to me. In doing this I was able to bury a little bit deeper all the issues I was trying to forget.

To everyone around me I was out of control, but on the inside, I was taking complete charge of everything. I knew that no one would ever take something from me again or tell me what to do or when to do it—the control would never again be ripped out of my hands. I would never again allow someone to dictate what happened to me and leave me there to pick up the pieces.

Oh No, Not Blue!

A few months had passed and I was getting more and more fatigued and found myself wanting to sleep all the time. I realized I was cutting school just to find somewhere to crash for a few hours. I would actually sleep at the elementary school playground or the neighborhood church parking lot–anywhere just to sleep. And I was getting sicker by the day. I couldn't manage to think about food before my stomach was doing flip-flops. The dark circles and bags under my eyes were becoming more and more noticeable. That's when I began to think the worst: I was either dying of some unknown illness or I was pregnant. It was by far one of the scariest thoughts for my fifteen-year- old mind to try and wrap around.

So I decided to buy a pregnancy test in hopes of solving this mystery, but praying to God that I just had some type of flu bug that would soon pass. I grabbed my twin sister Lisa, went into the bathroom, and locked the door. As I sat waiting for the results from the pregnancy test, I prayed and prayed for the stick not to turn blue...please, Lord, don't let it turn blue. A minute later I couldn't stand the anticipation any longer so I made Lisa look at the stick. The tip of the stick had turned bright blue. I was pregnant! I could not believe what was happening to me. I had just taken control of my life and now the control was once again being ripped away from me. This sent me spiraling downhill and out of control once again.

What in the world were my parents going to think? How was I going to tell them? I thought of running away. I thought of not telling them at all. Anything but telling my parents. I knew with this one simple statement I was about to disclose to them that it was going to shatter their world and make them feel like they had failed as parents. I was more hurt and saddened for them than to think of what in the world I was going to do with a baby at fifteen.

However, I did gather up the courage to tell them, but I couldn't even look at them as I uttered the words "I'm pregnant" because of the shame I felt. As my mom heard those words, she sat in shock for a moment that soon turned into overwhelming emotion of tears and sadness. As I watched the tears slowly well up in my daddy's eyes, I just knew that it was a moment I would never be able to erase from my memory. At that moment I was as broken as a person could be at the thought of what I had just done to them. I was willing to do or say anything to take away their pain and sadness, but there was nothing I could do. I had to just sit there and watch my parents be emotionally ripped to shreds right in front of me knowing I had caused it.

The next few months were very tense around my house, but eventually everyone seemed to get used to the idea of my pregnancy, which I was grateful for. But the further along I got in my pregnancy, more and more questions began swirling around in my head. What was I going to do about school? Was I going to try and continue my education after the baby came? Was I going to get my GED instead? How were my boyfriend and I going to handle parenting under different houses? How in the world was I going to make this work?

One afternoon when I was four and a half months pregnant, I was sitting outside with Alexander discussing what had happened during his football practice that day. I began feeling very tired, achy, and bloated. After suffering with it for a short time, I went inside and told my mom I wasn't feeling well and that I was cramping really badly. After talking with her for a few minutes I excused myself to go to the bathroom and couldn't believe what I was seeing. I was bleeding, a lot. I explained to my mom what was happening and she immediately put me in the car and raced me to the emergency room. With everything happening so fast I didn't even have the chance to think about what was going on.

After signing in at the hospital I was taken back and put in a hospital gown. The doctors began running their battery of tests as I was poked and prodded like a human pin cushion. I couldn't fully understand what was going on when the ultrasound technician kept asking me if I was sure I was pregnant. Every time she asked me, I replied yes. I couldn't understand why a nurse of all people would keep asking me if I was pregnant. I thought, You're the nurse, you should know. Just look at the ultrasound screen, stupid. And then reality hit me. I knew why she kept asking me. She couldn't see my baby on the ultrasound monitor screen.

It took them an entire day to confirm that my baby had died. My blood count went down dramatically when it should have doubled. Then the dreaded news came: they were scheduling me for a dilation and curettage (D&C) to remove my baby. I was beyond shocked. I didn't even fully understand what a D&C was let alone comprehend what was involved with it. When it was explained to me that it was a surgical procedure in which the cervix is dilated so that the uterine lining can be scraped to remove abnormal tissues, I just about lost it!

Why did my baby die? Was it something I had done? Something I hadn't done? The guilt was overwhelming because I suspected that all of my hard partying had something to do with the death of my unborn child even though I stopped all drug use the day I found out I was pregnant.

I had so many questions as I felt myself starting to slip into panic mode. I felt such a loss for my baby, which I'd only had for a short time. I hadn't even gotten the chance to feel it move. As I was trying to comprehend exactly what was going on, the doctor came in and put something into my IV and I drifted off to sleep. It seemed that every time I woke up someone was there pumping something into my IV, and at that point I welcomed the feeling of numbness.

I was so overtaken with grief that I didn't feel like I could express myself because I thought everyone else was secretly relieved that I hadn't ruined my life with a baby. I felt like I had to act like it was OK and that in the long run it was best for everyone. On the inside I was screaming, I'm mourning the death of my unborn baby–a baby I will never get the opportunity to hold, or to name, or to watch grow up.

Why did the last few months take place? Why did I have to get pregnant and shred every bit of trust my parents had in me? Have my friends find out and judge me just to have it ripped away instantly? Why did this happen? Why did an innocent baby have to die? There were so many unanswered questions.

It took a few months for the shock to wear off before I could really start to process what had happened. When the feelings and emotions came rushing in, I felt myself sinking back into that all too familiar black hole of depression that I had just been beginning to pull myself out of. I was scared to death because I didn't think I would be able to pull myself out of it again, and at this point, I didn't want to.

My Triplet...

Losing a child at any age, fifteen or fifty, whether it was a miscarriage, or you were fortunate enough to have the child with you for a period of time, has to be one of the hardest things a person will ever go through. I know the feeling of loss and it's like a little piece of you died right along with that child.

God may choose to show us the reasons why certain things happen in our lives, but some of our questions that we seek answers for may not come in this lifetime. We may have to wait until we get to heaven to ask God to provide us with those answers. I can't lie and say I like it, but I do trust Him. Peace may not come instantaneously, but if He is invited into your situation, I promise you that He will prove himself to be the Prince of Peace.

It took me a lot of wasted years and mistakes to figure out that you won't find that peace or comfort you're looking for in a bottle of alcohol, a cigarette, drugs, food, shopping, or sex. Or whatever form of numbing out a person uses to feel better.

The following is an example of how awesome He is even when things look to be the most helpless and grim.

In January 2007, after rededicating my life to the Lord and starting this journey of writing this book, my mom also reinstated her relationship with the Lord. I felt for the first time in my entire life like I finally had the relationship with my mom that I had always dreamed about. We were at the same place at the same time, a spiritual high. We clicked in a way I never thought possible. We had always been extremely close, but this was something much deeper. I enjoyed our relationship and appreciated her for who she was.

We would sit side by side every Sunday at church and I soon found myself looking at her in a completely different light; I was absolutely in awe of my mom. I wasn't looking at her like my mom, someone who gives advice when needed, or someone I talk to a few times a week, but I was looking at what an awesome, unique, and exciting person she was. How in the world had I not seen this before? You could have placed me beside a rock star or the president of the United States, anyone else in the world and I would not have chosen anyone different to be seated next to! I felt privileged to know her, to be friends with her, to call her mom. She was a woman I so admired and I wondered how I had spent my life not viewing her this way. I felt sad about the time I wasted not showing her how much she meant to me and wondered if she knew how crucial she was in my life. From that moment on I swore to myself that I would never be found guilty of not showing her every day how awesome I thought she was and what she meant to me.

As I was appreciating my newfound friendship with her, in March of 2007, she started experiencing some health issues. Mom decided to consult her family physician regarding pain she was having in her hip area. She had experienced pain in her hip for quite some time and it was getting to the point of her not being able to alleviate the pain. Sitting, standing, walking, and lying down were extremely painful for her.

At the first consultation she was examined and was told to go and get some X-rays completed to see what was going on. A few weeks later, she went back to the doctor to get her results and she was told she had a fractured pelvis and an abnormality in her hip joint. "Abnormality in the hip joint?" What in the world did that mean? My twin sister Lisa and I began joking with her telling her it was our triplet that had set up camp and thirty-five years later was ready to be born. We weren't too concerned because we thought it was a fracture that could be fixed with rest and rehabilitation.

She was sent for a bone scan of the hip and pelvis area. It came back that she did have a fractured pelvis and abnormal bone marrow. Abnormal bone marrow! Wasn't that cancer? Our "triplet" soon turned into a nightmare as the entire family grew panicked. A third test was ordered and she was sent for an MRI that confirmed that she did have abnormal bone marrow and was diagnosed with leukemia. I can't explain the shock and disbelief at the news we had just received. I couldn't fathom losing my mom and couldn't process the information I had just heard for fear of the outcome.

The depression that immediately crept back into my life was so familiar, I felt like someone was sucking the life right out of me. I began questioning God. I began with the simple question: Why God? Soon, a thousand more questions followed. How was our family going to survive the loss of our matriarch? How would Daddy survive the loss of his lifetime sweetheart? How would I fill the hole in my heart that no one else could possibly fill? After a few days of allowing the enemy to rock me to my core with every scary, depressing, and death- filled scenario, I felt the Lord's presence take over as He began changing my thought process to thinking of life instead of death.

So I did what I felt the Lord nudging me to do, I prayed. At this point, the entire family was praying and fasting for God to deliver her from the cancer. I can't tell you how many prayers were spoken over her and how many meals we fasted. A few days into our "project mom," God placed a feeling of peace in my soul that I just can't explain to the carnal mind. In my spirit I knew she was rid of the cancer. I knew without any explanation I could come up with that the Lord had already healed her. This was what the feeling of peace that passes all understanding truly means. I should have been worried, frantic, hopeless, and angry, but instead the Lord showed me firsthand what peace really meant.

A fourth test was ordered and she was sent for a full body bone scan to see if the leukemia had affected any other joints. We had to wait three and a half weeks for the results of that test. We all continued our prayers for her, but my prayers weren't for healing this time, they were for God to show her how big He really is. I prayed that through this incident she would have her faith increased by experiencing a true healing and miracle from God. I wanted Him to give her a story that could have come straight from the Bible.

Take that, Devil!

The night before she was to get her results back I was in my prayer closet when the Lord spoke to me and told me that I needed to be there for the reading of the results. I was to be with her and hear firsthand what the doctor had to say.

I know now why He wanted me to be there—so I could share this story with you. I tossed it back and forth in my mind because I knew my mom was a very private person and would probably want to do it alone, but I knew what the Lord had said to me. I didn't want to infringe on her privacy, but I also wanted to obey the Lord.

The next morning I got ready and headed over to the doctor's office. I walked into the waiting room and looked around to find my mom. I saw her sitting there reading a magazine. She looked like an impatient and scared little girl in a grown-up body. In that split second of seeing her sitting there I saw her as a helpless, frightened child. I had to fight back the huge lump in my throat to remain strong for her.

The look of complete shock on her face when she saw me walk in was priceless. I could tell she was trying to be strong, but I saw the look of fear in her eyes. As I made small talk with her, the nurse came out and called her back. She told me to wait in the waiting room for her but I stood up, grabbed my purse, and told her, "No, I'm going back with you."

We waited for the doctor, wondering if this process could possibly go any slower. It seemed like we were back there for three days when the doctor finally came in. I could tell my mom was getting fidgety. She just wanted the results, and she wanted them now. Every time the doctor would start reading the results, we were interrupted by a nurse coming in asking for information from the doctor. This happened a few times in the short few minutes she was in the room. Then she received a phone call and had to step out of the room. Our patience was definitely tested at this point. The doctor stepped out of the room to take her phone call and my mom couldn't wait any longer. She took a peek at her medical records and was trying to make sense of the medical terminology when the doctor walked back into the room.

The doctor began reading through the test results and was looking a little astonished at what she saw. She flipped to the first page of my mom's records and started from the beginning.

She told my mom that the X-rays had come back showing a fracture to the pelvis and an abnormality in her hip joint. She proceeded to say that the bone scan showed that she had abnormal bone marrow, and the third test from the MRI showed she had leukemia. The fourth and final test of the full body bone scan came back that not only did it not affect her other joints, but it was no longer prevalent in the hip joint. My mom and I looked at each other and I began to grin.

T he doctor said, "It disappeared. Things like that don't just disappear... the abnormality was there in all the test results, but now it's completely gone!" I think the doctor was as astonished as we were, so much so that the doctor sent her to a bone specialist to review the results and he too confirmed that it was no longer prevalent! Boom! A death blow to the Devil right then and there!

STUCK ON A ROLLER COASTER!

All of our prayers worked and God healed my mom! I cringe at the thought of what the outcome could have been had we not prayed and fasted. But sometimes you have to go through things to realize that you did in fact make it through. You didn't get stuck in a circumstance in which God abandoned you. He pulled you through it. Isaiah 66:9 says, "Do I bring to the moment of birth and not give delivery?" says the Lord.

When a woman is giving birth, she feels excruciating pain and exhaustion. She feels like that baby will never be born, but eventually after long hours of labor, no sleep, no food, and knowing if she has to endure this one more minute she will die, that's when the baby's head appears. After all of her hard work of labor and pushing, at last the baby is born. The pain that she was in eventually pays off when she holds that baby in her arms for the first time. She can't even remember the pain she was in two minutes ago. She actually tells herself that everything she just went through was worth it and she would do it again in a heartbeat. She sees that the baby did not get stuck in the birth canal forever; eventually at the right exact time the Lord delivered the baby.

But understand that even though God will always win and bring about beauty from ashes, the enemy will fight you every step of the way because he does not want to see you successfully praying and seeking the guidance of God in your circumstances. He wants you to fall flat on your face. But that is when you can look at the enemy and tell him that it was all worth it—the stretch marks, heartburn until you puke, sleepless nights, weight gain, food cravings at 2:00 a.m. and the mood swings! But that is when you can look at the enemy and tell him that it was all worth it – the stretch marks, heartburn until you puke, sleepless nights, weight gain, food cravings at 2:00 a.m. and the mood swings – because the Lord gave you an awesome gift in the end that you would not trade for the world.

It is the same thing when we struggle with our afflictions. We want it to be over because we are exhausted. We have fought the good fight of faith, and then we want God to spring into action like our very own action figure.

Our walk with God is the same way. After we go through the birthing process with whatever circumstance we may be facing, there is victory right around the corner. God allows us to go through some things only to bring us out of it stronger, more determined, and better off because of it.

You will actually get to the point when you feel it was a blessing to have gone through something so difficult. I know it sounds ridiculous. But trust me, God allows it because He knows what will benefit you in the long run. It will in some way benefit your ministry. Call that a prophetic word if you will, but I guarantee your trials, tribulations, and struggles will be used for His glory and your ministry. The pain you experience today ushers you one step closer to your victory!

I promise that you will find complete freedom if you continue on this journey with me and follow the Lord's prompting in your life.

I truly believe blessings are God's way of showing us that He is always there, walking each step with you, if you ask Him to! Don't get me wrong, we can't walk around every minute of every day with the feeling of goose bumps popping from a Holy Ghost shout-down session–that's not reality. That's like being on a roller coaster the first few minutes. It's awesome and fun and your stomach starts doing the flip-flop thing. We find it so extremely breathtaking. Nothing beats that feeling. But if you are stuck on the roller coaster longer than a few minutes you start feeling nauseated, your head starts to pound, and you just know if you don't get off the ride within the next few seconds the person sitting in front of you is going to wear your lunch!

Our walk with God is like that; it takes work. You have to drive to the amusement park, find a parking spot, stand in line for three hours, and finally you will get that two-minute whirlwind ride we find so exhilarating. But those two minutes are so worth all the prep work you did to get there. It's the same thing when you get a blessing from the Lord; it makes everything you went through worth it.

So when things look to be the darkest, the most impossible, and painful, remember that God is in control of everything, showing Himself to still be the "miracle man." The bright morning star only shines in the morning when it's the darkest and coldest out.

In today's society, we believe our lifesaving heroes are doctors, firefighters, police, etc., ... and they are; they are our everyday heroes. But when does God get the credit for saving someone's life or putting out the fires in our everyday life by making that last dollar stretch until payday, curing an incurable disease, putting the love back into a dead marriage, or having a drug addict lay the drugs down and serve God?

I'm sure you have experienced miracles in your everyday life. How about finding the energy to make it through another day when you're stressed out? Maybe you held your tongue with that co-worker who sits around telling dirty jokes only to find yourself witnessing about Jesus instead? Do you wonder how you made it through the entire week back and forth to work on a quarter tank of gas? Do you find yourself detoured on your way home from work feeling frustrated because it took you an extra twenty minutes to get home only to find yourself watching the news realizing there was a fatal accident that the Lord directed you away from? Do you stop and realize that your friend who you haven't heard from in over a year happened to call just to say "I was thinking of you" at the exact moment you found yourself ready to scream because of the anxiety you may have been feeling at that particular moment?

If we purposely focus on the everyday miracles, I guarantee God will never cease to amaze you with how frequently He is watching over you being your protector and shield with whatever the world throws your way. There are still miracles that occur every day. We just need to remember to thank the correct hero!

PULLING A PETER!

If you are anything like me, you can relate with me when I say I am the most impatient person alive! If I see it, I want it, and I want it now. When I'm shopping I almost can't wait to get to the checkout counter to pay for it. However, being a child of God has really taught me patience. Patience in knowing that during dry spells in my daily walk with God that He still loves me and He still listens to my prayers. It's during the quiet times without the goose bumps, without constant reaffirmation that He loves me that I have learned to trust Him entirely, trust that He is working behind the scenes, and orchestrating something I cannot fathom at the time. That's where faith comes into play. He knows when to step back in and let you feel his presence.

Imagine if someone walked around and told you every five minutes, "I love you; you mean the world to me." It would get pretty boring and actually kind of irritating. The Lord knows what you need and when you need it. He's going to let you walk a little on your own, kind of test the water a little bit, you know, what I call "pulling a Peter!" Wouldn't it be awesome to have the faith to actually get out of the boat and walk on water! Whew, it sounds good to read about, but imagine the fear Peter must have faced. But he did get out of that boat, didn't he? Because let's face it, the Lord did not draw us out of the boat to drown! Sometimes He calls us out of the boat to show us the amount of faith we actually do have.

Faith must be present to pursue your God-given calling. But it's up to you to decide what you are going to do with it. Whether it is listening to His voice telling you to stash a twenty dollar bill in someone's Bible or comforting someone in her or his time of need. You don't have to be a world-renowned preacher or a famous singer. Because if that were the case, I would have a microphone belting out songs every chance I had. He has given you your own gifts. My pastor, Pastor Tim Oldfield, once said, "God doesn't call the qualified, he equips the willing!"

Every person has a purpose to fulfill in Christ. Your gift may be encouragement, God's chosen words He wants you to convey to someone. Everyone loves to be encouraged and to feel needed, to feel that they have a purpose, because they do. Jeremiah 29:11 says "For I know the plans I have for you," declares the Lord, "plans to prosper you and not to harm you, plans to give you hope and a future."

No one is exempt from doing something for the Lord. So, if you are saying to yourself that you don't have a calling on your life or you're not talented in anything, God says something different. If you are still breathing, then it's not too late to do something to further God's Kingdom. We were created in His image, which is love, so why not start by encouraging one another?

I don't know about you, but I love receiving a random text or note from someone with an uplifting or encouraging word. It can totally change the atmosphere. How awesome do you feel when someone compliments you or tells you what a fantastic job you did, or how valued you are? However, a person's gift of encouragement is wasted if it never leaves his or her mouth.

It would be like someone giving you a brand-new Mustang convertible but leaving it in the driveway never to be driven. You polish it with only the best car wax, you have your little evergreen tree air freshener hanging from the rearview mirror, and you even pull a car cover over it when the possibility of rain occurs, but you never take it out for a spin. God doesn't just want you to take it out for a Sunday stroll, a test spin, or only for a special occasion. He wants you to put the top down, letting the wind blow your hair, crank up the music, sing like no-one is listening, and to drive like there is no tomorrow. He wants you to enjoy your gift(s) to the fullest extent possible.

It's amazing to see the power of words. The Bible says that we have the power of life and death with the words we speak. You can put a few words together to completely tear someone apart or uplift someone when needed.

In Matthew 12:36-37 it says, "But I tell you that men will have to give account on the Day of Judgment for every careless word they have spoken. For by your words you will be acquitted, and by your words you will be condemned."

Words are what make the world go around. By words the entire world was created. Genesis 1:3 says, "And God said, 'Let there be light,' and it was so." Job 37:6 says, "He says to the snow, 'fall on the earth,' and to the rain shower, 'be a mighty downpour.'" He commanded it with words, and it was so.

Genesis 1:6 says, "And God said, 'Let there be an expanse between the waters and separate water from water,' and it was so." Not only did he separate the waters, but He designed them to perfection. Job 38:11 says, ."..when I said, 'This far you may come and no farther; here is where your proud waves halt.' Wow! Are you kidding me? Think about that: God commanded where the water had to stop.

By words man was made, according to Genesis 1:26, "Then God said, 'Let us make man in our image,'" and it was so. So if we are made in His image, we have the same power with our words as He does. We must have faith and believe what we are speaking.

If God, our maker and savior, created everything with words, then why do we as a society put any less thought and effort into choosing the words we speak? Shouldn't ours be chosen more wisely? If we want to be like Him, shouldn't we also put as much faith into the words we speak as He did?

Matthew 12:34 says, " You brood of vipers, how can you who are evil say anything good? For the mouth speaks what the heart is full of." So if your heart is right, your words will represent that. It is one thing to pray, "Lord, please let me make it through another day without killing someone," or we can pray, "Lord, let me be a vessel you can work through to touch someone's life today that may not know you."

The words we pray to our Heavenly Father should be faith-filled words ready to penetrate the atmosphere, not just mindless chatter to feel like we have done some life-altering Christian duty because we spoke a few lifeless words.

If you can relate to the first prayer of "let me make it through another day without killing someone," then you can change it by asking God to reveal what is in your heart that makes you have a negative attitude. The first step to rewriting your story is realizing that there are changes that need to take place and allow God to reveal them to you. God is a gentleman; He is not going to step in and take over without being invited.

We can turn a person to God or away from God with the way we act and the words we speak. Let's ask ourselves, are we furthering the Kingdom or defacing Christ? The Bible says in James 3:3, "When we put bits into the mouths of horses to make them obey us, we can turn the whole animal." Isn't it amazing that our words have the power to change the atmosphere? You have the power to speak life over someone instead of death. That just blows my mind when I think of the power we possess. I don't know about you, but I want my words to edify people, to encourage them, to show them the love of Christ—not only in my words, but also my behavior.

Some of our friends and family may never step foot in a church. You may be the only "church" that someone sees. What are you showing that person? Sometimes being light in a dark place will be the only opportunity you get to show friends and family the love of God.

From this moment forward let's agree to be more mindful of the words we speak.

I invite you to pray this with me:

"Lord, I come to you on behalf of my attitude and my words. I thank you for helping me guard my tongue. Show me how to speak words that only uplift and encourage the very people you created and have put in my life. I thank you Lord for placing people in my path that may not know you and giving me Godly wisdom on how to display the love of Christ to them so that it draws people to you and not away from you. I ask all of this in the mighty name of Jesus, Amen."

MOZART STARTED SOMEWHERE...

It's easy to speak life into someone that we like, but what happens when God asks us to speak life into someone that absolutely irritates us? That person that always seems to get what you want? He or she always finishes first? He or she seems to receive the undeserved favor that you feel you should have gotten. How do you handle that? Do you sit with your friends and talk about her, ripping her to shreds only to make yourself feel better? Are you in the habit of pulling others down to make yourself appear superior? Or do you find yourself praying for that person, asking God to bless him in every aspect of his life? I guarantee that if you do the latter of the two, God will bless you so much you will be overwhelmed with what He has in store for you.

Trust me, I have done it and have witnessed firsthand what God will do when you pray for someone who, well let's just say, someone who would not be at the top of your Christmas card list. I found out that when I prayed for those individuals, I couldn't do enough for them. God had changed my mindset so much that I couldn't wait to give words of encouragement to them, or to see them happy, or to see something awesome happen in their life. The Lord not only answered my prayer for them, but also gave me everything that I had prayed on their behalf. So, go ahead, pray that million-dollar bonus check their way!

If you are not in the habit of speaking life over people, make that your first and foremost prayer today. Ask God to guide the direction of your words. Pray that God removes any bitterness and anger from your heart and shows you how to speak those words of life over others. If you're a Christian and don't speak those words of life over someone, who will?

Make it a priority to choose your words wisely. Let Christ shine so brightly through you that it makes people crave what you have, not run in the opposite direction. Act and speak as if God were standing right beside you, because He is!

The gift of encouragement is something we all can give. The Lord wants you to feel comfortable in your gift(s) and the only way to do that is to use them every day. You have to hone your skills and practice them to make them beneficial.

Take the example of music. My daughter, Jordan, is extremely gifted in music. She sat down and taught herself to play piano by sound. Once she got the basics down, she began to flow in the Spirit. She explained that it felt like the music was coming from her belly. That's an example of what it says in John 7:38, "Whoever believes in me, as Scripture has said, rivers of living water will flow from within them." Her gift is music. Had she not sat down the first time at a piano and started piddling with the keys, she may have never discovered her gift from God.

You have to put forth effort before God can show you what He can fully do with you. It's like trying to play the piano for the first time and wanting to play like Mozart; it's probably not going to happen. You first have to learn to read music, learn the keys, work the foot pedals, and practice, practice, and then practice some more. But I guarantee that if you put as much effort into perfecting your gift(s) that God has given you, God will do a lot of the work through you. Don't just look at the wooden box with black and white keys longing to play beautifully; take the time necessary to learn what you need to learn, practice what you need to practice, and relish in the fact that God found you special enough to give you such an awesome gift.

~ Another link has been broken ~

CHAPTER 4
DYING TO LIVE

AFTER ENDURING SO MUCH in the past few years with the drugs, drinking, the miscarriage, and depression, it had truly taken a toll on me mentally, physically, and emotionally. How was I only sixteen and feeling so lost and depressed and that life held nothing meaningful?

At this point, Satan was wreaking havoc on my mind, which led me to having suicidal thoughts. He somehow climbed in my head and made me think that my life meant so little that my friends and even my family would be better off without me.

I felt so extremely desperate due to the despair I felt, I thought there was nothing left for me to do but end my life. There were times when I would be driving and an overwhelming urge would hit me to drive my car off the road over a bridge.

My mind would play the pros and cons of suicide within a split second but I was unable to find the courage to follow through with it. Something kept me from doing what I really wanted to do, which was to end it all. I thought with my luck I would end up alive and paralyzed instead of the results I was looking for. So, as these thoughts continued to plague my mind, I thought of a way to end my life in a definite and less gruesome way: an overdose.

I knew I could get my hands on as much drugs as I wanted so I started the planning process and began my preparation to, once and for all, end the despair and anguish I felt every waking moment.

DYSON THE DEVIL!

So one night I went into my bedroom, locked the door, sat on my bed, and began writing my goodbye letters. I was like a possessed person. My hand couldn't keep up with my emotions as I wrote my sad, pitiful, pathetic letters. I was able to put on paper what I was screaming on the inside but did not have the courage to say out loud to anyone.

I explained the feelings of worthlessness, anxiety, anger, resentment, bitterness, self-torment, shame; a victim mentality. I did not feel special or important. Stupidity. Fear. Pity. Every lie that the Devil whispered to me, I wrote it on that paper. He had used me as a punching bag for the last time. I would no longer have to hear his evil little voice in my head. The black cloud and evil force that tormented me was once and for all going to get what it wanted: me.

I felt freer in that little bit of time, purging my emotions on that tear-stained paper than I had in years. It was like a cleansing for me to express my innermost thoughts without anyone judging me by telling me how selfish I was being. I knew that this would be the most selfish act I had ever committed, but the enemy's voice was so loud I couldn't hear anything else. I just heard the voices that kept screaming "Do it! Do it! Do it now!"

The more and more I wrote the more saddened I became. I thought that writing all this would make me feel better, but it didn't. It actually made me feel worse and more desperate. The terror that ran through my mind was excruciating because not even the contemplation of suicide was making the pain disappear. It only added to my frustrations. Not only was I too miserable to live, but I became too scared to die.

I began bargaining with those voices in my head to shut up and let me think for a minute so I could finish writing my letters. I told myself that I was going to follow through with what I started–I just needed a little more courage. The voices kept screaming at me, telling me that I didn't need more courage just a backbone to finish it. They screamed at me to stop writing my senseless letters that no one would care about anyway and just finish it!

Before downing the entire bottle of pills, I chose to take only a few pills so I could focus on my written pros and cons list. My pros list meant I would follow through with the suicide and my cons list meant I would stay and suffer through life. It was amazing to see that very long list of pros and only a few on the cons side. I felt so extremely pathetic and this only reaffirmed my determination to end my life.

So I continued writing my letters feeling very panicked at the thought of what I was about to do when I found myself writing the letter to my mom and dad. I began thanking them for what they had stood for as good Christian parents. I apologized for everything I had put them through and tried to explain that none of this was their fault and how they would be better off without me because of the pain I always seemed to cause them.

And suddenly I began to sob; it was like a floodgate opened up. I wanted this letter to say everything about how I felt about them. It had to be perfect because I only had one shot at it and I didn't want to leave anything out.

That's when I heard a different voice inside my head, and this time there was no static and chaos. The voice I heard said, "I still love you." My hands were sweating and shaking uncontrollably as I sobbed hysterically with the tears just flowing down onto my letter.

I felt so unlovable and unworthy that I couldn't believe what I was hearing deep inside my soul. Was I really loved but so blinded by self- pity that I couldn't see it? Had self-pity taken over so much that I wasn't seeing the true reality in life?

I had sunk as low as I had ever been. My mind began to race, wondering what to do next– listen to the soft, kind, and loving voice inside my head, or follow through with what I had started. The thoughts waffled back and forth for a minute and then the voices that were "static chaos" got louder and louder in my head.

I reached over for the bottle of pills wanting the courage to follow through with it and to stop the screaming voices. I thought of taking a few more pills, but for some reason I didn't. I was stopped dead in my tracks. I was frozen. So, I just sat there wallowing in my own self-pity and tears.

I literally felt like someone grabbed a hold of me and pulled me away from the edge of the cliff I was so desperately trying to throw myself off of. I sat on my bed trying to make sense of what I was experiencing. But there wasn't a logical explanation.

I did not understand exactly what was happening, but I was grateful for the mental break. The screaming voices suddenly stopped. The static stopped. The fear was gone. There was no more chaotic darkness. There was no more panic. There was no more anything. I felt, nothing. This felt good. The tormenting boogeyman was gone! It's like something or someone came in that room and sucked him away in a sweeper. For the first time in years I felt free. I knew somehow with certainty that the loving voice I heard deep inside had caused the other voices to stop and I was grateful for it.

Needless to say, I didn't continue writing those good-bye letters. I didn't fully understand at the time why I put the letters away, but I did. I kept them under my mattress for a very long time and eventually threw them out. But when I did get rid of them, it was closing a chapter that I knew I never wanted to revisit, no matter what life threw my way.

HE IS ALL THAT!

It's "Godronic" because even then I knew it was God who had seen my time of need and had spoken words to me that turned my life around. He showed me that a person has a choice of which voice they choose to hear the loudest.

He placed something in my spirit that changed my whole thought process and I was able to be hopeful instead of helpless. Only God was able to keep me from making the biggest mistake of my life. He was that calm, loving, voice deep inside of me that brought clarity at the exact moment that I needed Him the most.

Proverbs 18:24 says, "One who has unreliable friends soon comes to ruin, but there is a friend who sticks closer than a brother." When no one else was there with me behind closed doors, He was there with me. He was the peanut butter to my jelly, the mac to my cheese, the butter to my bread. He is always there to flavor whatever we give him access to.

He is there with you, too. When you feel alone, He is there. When you want to hurt yourself, He is there. When you feel like no one cares or understands, He is there. When you feel abandoned, He is there. When you feel scared and paralyzed with fear, He is there.

Deuteronomy 31:8 says, "The Lord himself goes before you and will be with you; he will never leave you nor forsake you. Do not be afraid; do not be discouraged." So if the Lord is telling you that you shouldn't be afraid or discouraged, don't you think He has your back? I mean, c'mon friends, He is the winner of the biggest battle in the history of man, defeating our enemy and conquering death, Hell, and the grave! Don't you think He can handle your situation beautifully? He can, and He *will!*

Sometimes I feel we are all a little guilty of putting God in a small box when we tell Him how big our problems are instead of telling our problems how big our God is!

Come on, get excited with me! The Master of the Universe, the

Lion of Judah, the Prince of Peace, the Resurrected King, the Savior of the World, the Lamb of God, Emmanuel, the Anointed One, the Alpha and Omega, the Great Physician, the High Priest, the Divine Teacher is waiting for you to trust Him with your problems, your emotions, and your entire being.

There is *the* defining moment when you put all trust and faith into God, and that is when the fun truly begins. That's when the veil is lifted and you see clearly for the very first time! So c'mon and open those big beautiful eyes of yours and see what God has in store for you!

GOD...THE MIRACLE MAN!

Let's take a look at the story in II Kings of the widow and oil to see how God worked a miracle with the little she was given.

II Kings 4:2-6 says, "Elisha replied to her, 'How can I help you? Tell me, what do you have in your house?' Your servant has nothing there at all, (emphasis added)" she said, "except a small jar of olive oil." Elisha said, "Go around and ask all your neighbors for empty jars. Don't ask for just a few. Then go inside and shut the door behind you and your sons. Pour oil into all the jars, and as each is filled, put it to one side." She left him and shut the door behind her and her sons. They brought the jars to her and she kept pouring. When all the jars were full, she said to her son, "Bring me another one." But he replied, "There is not a jar left." Then the oil stopped flowing.

You see, what she thought was nothing actually turned out to be what God used to provide her miracle. That "nothing" of yours in God's hands is more than enough. Let's face it friends, you won't be given a miracle unless you need one. It's never fun to walk the road of poverty, or humility, or tribulations, or loss, or addiction. But how awesome is it when God shows up and provides you with exactly what you need, when you need it? He's just good and on time that way!

The oil didn't run out until there were no more vessels it could be poured into. We can also take this in the context of the vessels being us and the oil being the Lord's anointing. He filled every jar she had. When she asked for another jar, her sons told her there weren't anymore. That's when the oil stopped. You see, her miracle was sitting on a shelf collecting dust. The oil isn't the miracle. The jars aren't the miracle. The faith that God will do what He said he will do with the oil...that's the miracle! Now that's a sermon I could preach on for about seven weeks! Until you give God your "something" you don't know what miracle God has in store for you.

God will never shortchange a situation, leave something undone, or not meet you exactly where you are. He is concise and perfect in all He does. He has shown Himself as Jehovah Jireh, the Provider, time and time again.

Remember the story in Matthew 14:13-21 of the two fish and five loaves of bread that fed five thousand men? Jesus told them to bring the food to him and he gave thanks over it and gave it to the disciples to hand out. After everyone ate and was full, they cleaned up twelve baskets of scraps. Twelve baskets!

In this story, they started with what probably wouldn't feed a large family of five people, let alone five thousand. Yet they ended up with *more* bread than they started with! In our carnal minds I know you are thinking the same thing I did: how in the world is that possible? But God not only fed them, He gave them more than enough. He multiplied the "something" He was given and provided a miracle.

What about in Exodus 14 when the Red Sea was divided so the Israelites could walk over on dry land? God said, "But lift up your rod, and stretch out your hand over the sea and divide it." What if Moses had said, "Why in the world would God ask me to use this wooden rod, there is no power in it?" But Moses' faith wasn't in the rod itself, it was in God's words. Moses showed faith in believing God by *raising his rod.* That's when the sea split and they did indeed cross over on dry land. God used the "something" He was given and provided a miracle.

There are so many stories in the Bible to reference when it comes to miracles that it's hard to choose just a few. There were miracles in which God raised people from the dead, healed blinded eyes, and made the lame to walk. The list is endless. Faith, coupled with action, is the common denominator displayed in each story. As James 1:22 says, "Do not merely listen to the word…Do what it says." Faith must be in tandem with action! But what is the same in every story is an element of faith that was displayed. In tandem with faith there has to be action!

The widow woman acted by collecting the jars. She displayed action and faith. Jesus and the disciples gathered what they had and gave thanks for it. He acted and displayed faith. Moses' action was raising his wooden rod; he acted and had faith. In the stories I just referenced you can see that each person took some sort of action that showed their faith.

Do you want to see Bible-sized miracles? I know I do! Then let's give God our "something" and have faith that He will do what He said he would do. We can then sit back, relax, and watch what God does. I guarantee He will absolutely shock you with what He will do when you trust Him completely.

You Are Not Fried Chicken!

Are you in need of a miracle? Are you like the widow woman with absolutely nothing but a small jar of oil? Are you looking for that medical diagnosis to change miraculously? How about that dead marriage to come to life again? Do you want to be free of that depression and anger you have carried around your entire life?

You see, if you are breathing, it is probably safe to say that you could use a miracle in one aspect of your life or another. Because we live in a fallen world, the Bible says in 1 Peter 5:8, "Be alert and of sober mind. Your enemy the Devil prowls around like a roaring lion looking for someone to devour." Just because the Devil prowls around looking for someone to devour does *not* mean he can feast on you, My Friend. You are not fried chicken!

When you feel your faith slipping and you can't conjure up a fighting word on your own behalf, pray this little prayer to dispatch the Lion of Judah to your side and rest in the fact that you have the Master of the Universe fighting for you:

> *"Dear Heavenly Father, I come to you requesting to speak to the very heart of who you are. You know the circumstances I am facing and what my struggles are. I know you are bigger than my problems and you have already dispatched angels on my behalf to go before me to set off the trap the enemy has placed before me. Fight for me, Lord, and strengthen my faith when I can't see the physical manifestation of what you are doing in this situation. I rest in the fact that I know you have already perfected this and worked everything out for my good. Thank you, Lord. Amen."*

Your prayers are your action. Your faith means resting in the fact that He will answer you. It may not be how you expected Him to, but He will always answer. Congratulations! You have just learned a key element in fighting this spiritual war.

~ Another link has been broken ~

CHAPTER 5
GOD'S TWELVE-STEP PROGRAM

WHILE MY PAST SERVED AS a jumbled holding ground for brokenness, even after feeling the Lord so prevalent throughout the years, I was not able to break the pattern long enough to make a permanent change to quit the lifestyle I had grown accustom to and follow after Him. I just didn't find myself worthy enough to want more for myself, so I kept with my comfortable but unhealthy lifestyle that I was living in.

After several years, which spanned from my teenage years through my mid-thirties, I was habitually drinking and partying, trying not to deal with life. It was difficult to see what my self-destructive behavior had created.

Within a few short years of living the lifestyle I indulged in, I had created financial difficulties that led to a bankruptcy, failed relationships that led to failed marriages, anger issues, bitterness, and resentment all leading up to the realization that I was an alcoholic! Me, an alcoholic. Boy that tasted as bitter as moonshine coming off the tongue!

I was barely thirty years old with two kids and on the last leg of another failed marriage when this horrible epiphany took place.

What led me to realizing I had an addiction to alcohol is when I would try to wait to start drinking until the kids were in bed. I didn't succeed very often. In fact, I can't remember a time that I did succeed. I would make myself feel better by telling myself, "I am just unwinding and it's OK to drink a few if I don't get drunk." The problem was I never realized that I was drunk when I was in fact, drunk.

No matter what I told myself about not drinking I always found some excuse to start drinking. I was so selfish in thinking I was only hurting myself and that I wasn't hurting my kids. I was so fixated on my own need for a buzz, and to be numb, I didn't realize how much they were probably being hurt by my drinking. I told myself time and time again, I'll be better tomorrow. I won't start drinking until they go to bed so they won't see me. But I would start having those uncontrollable thoughts in my head and before I knew it, I was twisting the cap off of a beer ready to start drinking. It's amazing how our thoughts soon lead to becoming our actions. This is where the Devil plants his slimy seeds, in our thoughts.

I would start playing mind games with myself. I would tell myself that if I could go ahead and have a drink that I would actually be a better mom and that I would be able to handle their fighting and arguing if only I could get that one drink in me. I would be able to focus more. I actually got to the point that I thought I was doing them a favor if I had a drink or two in me because I wasn't so mean and edgy when I had a buzz. I was slowly realizing I was doing a lot more yelling and screaming at them than actual "real parenting." This was a tough realization to have as a mom.

Out of guilt I began arguing with myself saying, *I am an adult and I am allowed to have a drink and any kid who doesn't understand that doesn't understand what it's like to be a grown up with grown-up problems.* I couldn't believe I was rationalizing my actions. I had actually sunk so low that I was blaming my children for the guilt I was feeling. I blamed my past circumstances and my present circumstances, and then realized I was placing a lot of blame instead of seeing the situation for what it really was: I was an alcoholic.

That was a hard mirror to look in, and what an ugly site I saw. I had to physically say it out loud to believe it. But was I? I didn't wake up every morning and down a fifth of Vodka. I didn't sneak it throughout the day. I didn't steal for it. I just drank in the evenings. I was a "functioning alcoholic."

I cooked dinner every night. I did the laundry. I helped the kids with homework. I mowed the grass. I did what was expected of me all while I had my handy dandy drink in my hand. But did that make me an alcoholic? Was that label for me? I answered my own questions when I made these realizations: Was anyone being affected by my alcohol consumption? Yes. Was I feeling the need to sneak and lie about my drinking? Yes. Could I go one day without drinking or even thinking about it? Absolutely not.

I sat on my living room floor with my face buried in my hands and bawled like a little girl. I was like a lifeless rag doll sitting there wondering how I became a person I didn't even recognize. How did life get so complicated? How was I going to make things right with my babies of seven years old and four years old? Then the real panic set in when I asked myself, how am I going to stop drinking?

At that moment of realization I felt like someone was dying. I couldn't figure out what this dark and depressing emotion was that just washed over me. It was a disgusting and putrid feeling. It was all over me. It was every demon in Hell holding on for dear life; they knew they were being served with their walking papers and being evicted!

I can only imagine what kind of war was going on in the spiritual realm. Maybe I would have seen God going to the battle line for me to fight off the spirit of addiction. Fighting off the spirit of pity. Fighting off the spirit of bitterness, anger, rage, resentment, victimization, depression, and loneliness. They all had to go. And it started with the spirit of alcoholism!

I would have given anything to hear the enemy screaming in fear because of what was about to take place: it was time to fight! My mindset began to shift and I knew I was in the fight of my life. I thought, *Let the war begin!*

No More Labels!

When this realization took place, I was so scared because I didn't know how to fight this demon. This was unfamiliar territory for me. I felt guilt for several months while recognizing that tugging in my heart and the familiar voice asking me to come home. It was God preparing me to return to Him, and to secure my salvation.

I remember Him reaching out to me in so many different ways during that time. One way was being surrounded with an entire Christian family that continued to pray for me daily. I remember seeing a billboard sign leaving a party one night that read, "Jesus Saves." Then I heard a Christian song on a secular station. The song I heard was, *"I Can Only Imagine."* I can only imagine, really? I can only imagine that I am not hearing this song on a secular radio station! I thought, *OK God, I hear you.* Tears rolled down my cheeks as I heard the lyrics to that song and I just knew I had to turn my life around.

A week before I rededicated my life to God back in 2007, I told Him that if He would give me the willpower to stop drinking, I would serve Him every day of my life with the same force I had served the enemy. You know what? He did.

I knew I was going to attend Church the next Sunday to give my life back to God, but with what labels? I was horrified thinking that my new label was going to be "alcoholic." What would people think? How would I live a sober life and feel normal in it?

But God showed me that all my life I had labeled myself as an alcoholic, a rape victim, a backslider, so why carry around a label of what I had been before being a born-again Christian? It was society's label, not a label for one of His children.

Does a person who used to be a thief announce to everyone, "Hi, my name is Carletta. I was a thief before I got saved and I probably stole from you or someone you know, but anyways, how the heck are ya?" No! So I didn't accept that title or label for myself.

I will be the first person to admit that I viewed my past behaviors and state of mind as disgusting and pathetic. But through the grace of God He washed every bit of that away so I don't have to carry around the ugly title of "alcoholic."

I believe that is Satan's way of beating us down every chance he gets. It's his little way of keeping his foot on our throat. I will not allow Satan to remind me of the negative things I once did, and neither should you! If we allow him to remind us of our past, then how in the world can we walk forward?

I prayed about whether I should attend an Alcoholics Anonymous twelve-step program or something that would help me close that chapter in my life. But the Lord showed me that He had already laid out my twelve-step program. It's called the Twelve Tribes of Israel. Each tribe is a step in the right direction to freedom and to the Promised Land.

The more and more I researched the Twelve Tribes of Israel, I was shocked and in complete disbelief about what I uncovered. Bear with me; I promise this gets extremely interesting.

I am going to list each tribe name in the order of when each son was born and provide you with the meaning of each name. I'm then going to share with you my notes from my personal journal I kept as I went through my "drying out" process. The notes may not be complete in thought content because it was for my own personal records...or so I thought. I had no clue that the Lord would want me to publish them in a book.

While reading the following journal entry, remember that this also applies to you. If you are in need of dropping that old habit or addiction, the first step is to acknowledge that you want change and freedom from it.

I am going to *italicize* below what I believe will help us recognize what the Lord wants us all to acknowledge and how we can break free from our addictions. If this doesn't apply to you, I still invite you to follow along to further your knowledge on how to help someone else that may be in your social circle who is fighting an addiction or searching for freedom.

Keep in mind, I wrote my personal journal entries weeks before God directed me to study the Twelve Tribes of Israel.

First-born son, Reuben: Meaning: my misery; first sign of strength

(My personal journal notes) Jan 1, 2007–Day 1- "First day without alcohol. Feel very helpless and wonder why I listened to God, having serious thoughts of having just one drink, can't believe how difficult this is. Want so much to turn back, it is too hard. People drank in the Bible, I can too...how in the world am I going to do this? I feel a nudging on the inside to keep going. So that's what I'm going to do, I'll keep going, but man this sucks."

"Steps to Sobriety"

*Acknowledge your problem and see the detrimental effects it has on you and your life. Decide **today** to start your new journey of complete freedom from your addiction.*

Second-born son, Simeon: Meaning: take heed; listen

(My personal journal notes) Jan 2, 2007–Day 2 – "God is showing me different ways of dealing with the withdrawal by reading uplifting scriptures and listening to my Christian music. "I can do all things through Christ who strengthens me" is becoming one of my favorites.

I'm trying not to feel sorry for myself, but it's hard because that's what I have always done."

"Steps to Sobriety"

*Listen to the Lord's voice **only**. Keep in mind the enemy will come to you speaking so many lies, but keep your focus honed in on God's promises to you. He says He will never leave you nor forsake you.*

Third-born son, Levi: Meaning: joined; attached

(My personal journal note) Jan 3, 2007–Day 3 – "I know I will never turn back. Something broke in me and I know I have conquered the addiction. God is showing me that I don't have to suffer weeks or months going through withdrawal. I am so special to God that He is showing me different ways that He is here with me fighting. I am now just processing the mind games and the old lifestyle habits."

"Steps to Sobriety"

God states that He has you in the palm of His hand, that He has the very hairs on your head numbered, if you abide in Him, then He abides in you. He is fighting for you today because He loves you.

Fourth-born son, Judah: Meaning: praised

(My personal journal note) Jan 4, 2007– Day 4 – "Feeling very strong and thanking God for taking away my urges. The song *"Call On Jesus"* from Nicole C. Mullen came on the radio a little bit ago and I thought I was going to have a Holy Ghost fit right here in the kitchen. Go God! I can't wait for church on Sunday!"

"Steps to Sobriety"

God encamps around our praise, so go ahead and shout a hallelujah. If you are struggling today, sing a song, tell the Lord how much you love Him, remember, our praise scatters the enemy.

Fifth-born son, Dan: Meaning: God has judged me and heard my voice; vindicated

(My personal journal note) Jan 5, 2007–Day 5 – "There is nothing I can't do with God on my side. I feel like the last few days have been the hardest, easiest, longest, and shortest, and I have experienced the most mind-blowing epiphanies ever. God seems to answer me before the last word has left my tongue. Crazy how much He is carrying me through this whole thing. Mind blown!"

"Steps to Sobriety"

God has seen your struggles. He hears your cries and He hears your praises. He has cleared your name and made your name great! He is telling you to celebrate because you have victory.

Sixth-born son, Naphtali: Meaning: my struggle

(My personal journal note) Jan 6, 2007–Day 6 – "Today I feel a sense of loss of my old life and habits. I feel like someone died! This is by far the worst day so far...I think even more than day one. I don't understand it. For the first time in forever I am "feeling" and can't numb out and take the pain away. I have to feel everything and deal with it the best I can. I have to break habits, emotionally, physically, and mentally. I have to say good-bye to the life I once knew. Crying a lot today because I don't know what I am going to see in the mirror with a sober view! Am I going to like the new me? Will people still think I'm fun and the life of the party? Ugh, I wanna go back to bed!"

"Steps to Sobriety"

When the enemy comes to steal your joy, your victories and your praises, you tell him that the Lion of Judah has been dispatched out before you to meet him at the battle line! Rest in the fact that you have a conquering King fighting for you.

Seventh-born son, Gad: Meaning: good fortune

(My personal journal note) Jan 7, 2007–Day 7 – "Went to church today and made it official. I rededicated my life to God! I think that doing a public show of my heart change is something from my childhood. God knows where my heart has been, though. So happy today, but don't understand how I was so happy at church just to come home and feel so...blah. I feel very depressed today but trying to look on the bright side of how far I have come. Having serious mood swings. One minute I am crying and the next I am singing worship songs...sort of freaking myself out thinking God took all my numbing medicine away and left me here to deal with a crazy person. Wondering what kind of person I am going to be. What is He going to have me do to further

His kingdom? Maybe a singer? Ha ha, not likely! Well it seems like I'm at least getting my sense of humor back! That's a good sign. I am still funny without alcohol! Who knew!"

"Steps to Sobriety"

Your fortune is a spiritual force that is affecting the very outcome of your success. Smile and know that God is holding your hand walking with you toward the finish line! Don't give up!

Eighth-born son, Asher: Meaning: fortunate, happy

(My personal journal note) Jan 8, 2007– Day 8 – "I'm starting to feel like I have been through a war, but on the winning side of the battle line. It makes sense in my head even though I don't understand it fully. I'm coming around, realizing I probably have made it through the worst part. Feeling a sense of accomplishment today and stronger than I have in years. I'm on my way. I'm actually "feeling" today and I'm OK with it. I'm happy with my decision to start this journey. My song *"Shackles"* came on the radio and I about danced myself into a heart attack...ha ha."

"Steps to Sobriety"

The joy of the Lord is your strength. Delight in the Lord for He is extremely pleased with you.

Ninth-born son, Issachar: Meaning: he is hired; felt reward

(My personal journal note) Jan 9, 2007– Day 9 – "I know that I could not have done what I have just been through without God! Feeling very proud of myself today. Keeping the Word pouring in to me... I feel like that's been my saving grace. I actually quoted a scripture from memory today. It's the small things that tickle me!"

"Steps to Sobriety"

Today is a day to celebrate and look at everything you have accomplished. Focus on your strengths and how far you have come.

Tenth-born son, Zebulun: Meaning: dwelling; great honor

(My personal journal note) Jan 10, 2007– Day 10 – "Feeling like the best mom in the world today. Jordan came up and wrapped her arms around my neck and said I was the best mommy ever! Wow. God is bringing restoration all the way around. All the horrible things I felt about myself being a bad mom when I was drinking is fading away and being replaced with these kind of memories."

"Steps to Sobriety"

There is new identity surfacing. Take some time to reevaluate how you view yourself, and how the Lord views you.

Eleventh-Born Son, Joseph: Meaning: may he add; taken away my disgrace

(My personal journal note) Jan 11, 2007– Day 11 – "The shame of who I was before is drifting away. Feeling comfortable in standing up for myself and the things I want for myself now. I realize I really like the person I saw in the mirror this morning. I realized today how truthful of a person I was years ago...no need to lie now because I can remember every detail of every situation. Yay! God is restoring me all the way around. Something I didn't even think about until today, but He did. My kids adore me. I'm sober. I'm honest. Getting excited to think about the new and improved Lori!"

"Steps to Sobriety"

Now that the new identity of yourself has surfaced, your old self and mindset will start fading away. Every day is a new day to fulfill and accomplish anything you set your mind to.

Twelfth-born son, Benjamin: Meaning: son of the right hand

(My personal journal note) Jan 12, 2007– Day 12 – "I am looking ahead at the new me, the new person God has brought about. I can't believe God has taken away not only my drinking urges but my view of my old self... I actually love the new me! No more deceit, no more short fuses, no more! This war I have been through the last several days has allowed my old self to die. It was hard and I wanted to quit, but God carried me through. Thank you, Lord, for bringing me through one of the hardest things I have been through."

"Steps to Sobriety"

Your hard work has paid off and you have conquered what you have set out before you. Allow the old habits to fall by the wayside and walk freely in your new found freedom. Be proud of yourself!

Let me just say that I was amazed at how the Twelve Tribes of Israel lined up so perfectly with what I went through. The meaning of each name, in the order of their birth and my journal entries, corresponded exactly.

If you have reached the point in your life where you are tired of living with an addiction, then now is your time to be free from it. Let's keep in mind that the Lord cannot fix what He is not given. But if you are ready to be rid of it, I suggest that you acknowledge your addiction and your weaknesses that come from it and put God in complete charge of your addiction. This means trusting Him to help you walk through the process, whatever your process may look like. He will never ask you to go somewhere where He isn't present. He will never ask you to do it alone. He will never ask you to give Him something He isn't capable of handling.

Once you have made your decision to give it all to God, set your "quit date" and *don't* waiver with it. I strongly suggest that you pray and fast (meaning to abstain from something) until your quit date and ask God to give you the strength to follow through with quitting your addiction. Remember, when you are weak…that is when HE is strong. You **can** do this, you are much stronger than you think you are!

Write down what your "triggers" are and have and "exit" plan in mind before you start your process. This way when you are tempted and your mind is clouded with confusion and the enemy is lying to you, you will know how to handle the situation. This is something I found to be extremely helpful because the enemy will not sit idly by and watch his handiwork (you) just slip away. But don't let that scare you! You have the Lion of Judah on your side and He has already won the biggest battle in the history of man; with Him walking hand in hand with you, you can't fail! But you can't do this in your own strength, or you would have already done so. You **must** lean on the Lord through this process, because that is where victory is won.

I strongly suggest you journal your daily progress. Some days are going to be easy, some days you will have to fight like Evander Holyfield to keep your addiction far away from you. But if you decide to do a journal, you will see little nuggets along the way that the Lord shared with *only* you. You will have your very own roadmap to show you how big our God is and what He walked you through. While going through this process, remember that Romans 8:18 says, "I consider that our present sufferings are not worth comparing with the glory that will be revealed in us." Your freedom *is* worth fighting for!

The Lord showed me while going through this process that I was a little bit like Abraham waiting for my promised seed. I was the three Hebrew children in the fiery furnace. I was Job that was tormented and still waited upon the Lord. I was Peter who got out of the boat. I was Joshua who was bold and courageous. But I was also Thomas who doubted a little bit.

You see, it's OK to be a little scared while going through your storm, or while you're getting your breakthrough. But that's the key: getting your breakthrough. You will not stay in the place where you are right now. And for those of you who are resting on your mountaintop and want to stay where you are, I know you want to slap me right about now because those mountaintop experiences and times with the Lord are what make life worth living.

A friend of mine asked me, "If God can take it all away with a snap of His finger, why didn't He? Why did He make you suffer while you were giving up your addiction?" I explained to my friend that by doing it His way and in His timeframe He was able to strengthen my faith and trust in Him. But to be honest, the biggest lesson I learned was realizing my *need* for Him. Because let's face it, if I could have done it on my own without Him, I would have.

I began thinking about all the miracles Jesus performed that I had read about in the Bible, but what He did for me was bring me through to my own miracle and each day I got stronger and stronger.

It's like winning the lottery. Of course, it would be awesome to receive that huge unexpected sum of money, but how much more do you appreciate each and every dollar when you go out and sweat and labor twelve hours a day for that money? I'm certain you would hold on to that money a little bit tighter and appreciate it a little bit more.

You will find yourself appreciating the hard work God allows you to go through to show you how strong you are when you rely on Him. And I needed that confirmation of how strong I could be if I trusted in Him. God knew I needed thick skin to get through the things He was going to allow me to go through. And who knew He would turn this once-alcoholic into an author. That's *my* AA story.

What will your story be when you give God your everything? I'm certain it will be something so magnificent that it will shock even you.

JESUS OUR JANITOR?

When you are the one facing the war, it seems so much bigger, scarier–and quite honestly–more demonic! Why is that? Do you think physical, mental, emotional, or spiritual warfare is the worst? I'm sure that whatever kind of warfare you're facing right now is the answer you just gave to my question.

Why is it that Carrie's lack of $25 for groceries this week seems so much worse to her than Taylor's son being deployed to war? I will tell you why. It is because she is the one going through the battle.

What about Erika and her diagnosis with breast cancer? She thinks her pain is by far the worst; the chemo treatments, the puking for hours, sometimes for days after treatment. The constant battle to find new veins to poke is breaking her in two. After the physical pain takes a toll on her, then there is the loss of her hair, and her fear of becoming less and less attractive to her husband. She is too tired to play with her kids in the backyard. She wonders if she will live long enough to see her daughter walk down the aisle to her prince charming.

Terri definitely wins hands down, right? She has been tormented her entire life by her abusive father from as far back as she can remember. He beats her and then apologizes and begs her for forgiveness. Of course, he promises to never let it happen again, and then two days later, he repeats it. This leads to her promiscuous behavior to help numb her emotions. She allows every man she comes in contact with to abuse her physically and sexually. Somehow in her mind that equals love. She soon starts turning tricks on the streets to pay for her out-of-control drug addiction. This all wreaks havoc on her physically, mentally, and emotionally.

Now Bev suffers from the little voices in her head. No matter what she does, she can't get rid of them. She drinks, smokes, starts doing drugs, anything to get rid of them. Why are they telling her to do things she knows is wrong? Her mental state almost can't hold on anymore. The decision process for choosing right and wrong is becoming more clouded and unclear. She tries to get rid of the mental anguish she feels every waking moment, but nothing helps until she tries a food binge. Oh, wait a minute, she starts to feel better; food is the ticket! It helps temporarily while the food is in her mouth, but then the darkness soon creeps back in; until the next food binge. But now she is 160 pounds overweight. Mentally, physically, and emotionally she is slipping away.

What do you see in these situations that all resemble one another? Not one time in all the dilemmas do you see anything mentioning the spiritual side of the situation. Do you think it would have helped? If Carrie, Taylor, Erika, Terri or Bev had called upon the Lord for help, do you think it would have changed their situation?

Do you see the pattern? Mental, physical, and emotional pain are all equal; not one type of pain is more painful than the other. In all of these scenarios there isn't one instance in which one type of pain didn't somehow intertwine with the others. Physical pain will inevitably lead to mental and emotional pain. The same thing will happen with mental pain leading to emotional and possibly physical pain. It's a vicious cycle that keeps going and going and going, like that stupid Energizer Bunny...This is one time that the drum-beating bunny is not so cute!

I do believe that if the Lord had been given the opportunity, He could have helped in all those situations. The problem is, He wasn't even invited to the party. He wasn't the guest of honor, or a special VIP, or even a party attendee. He was asked to come to the party only to be a janitor. He was asked to come and clean up our mess.

Sometimes, I think we as carnal beings get so caught up in our own chaotic situation and striving to keep from drowning in our own mess that we forget to invite the Lord into our mess.

Funny how we do that, isn't it? I'm not preaching at you, I'm also holding that unwanted mirror in front of my face as well. I think we all have been found guilty of trying to fix our own mess without asking the Lord for help. I have done that so many times, and then found myself kicking and screaming like a five-year-old little girl wondering why God allowed something bad to happen.

I would cry my big crocodile tears asking Him where He was in my situation. "Lord, I thought you were supposed to keep me safe. You were supposed to keep the boogeyman away. You were supposed to keep this from happening to me." Then I would clearly hear Him say, "If you didn't keep me locked outside like a janitor in the broom closet, Baby Girl, I could have told you that first of all, I love you. I am your greatest strength when you use me in your situation and fully trust in me. My willingness to set you free from whatever bondage you are in will absolutely amaze you. But you have to learn to put me *before* your mess, not after it."

What about you? Are you being tested on every side? Are you being asked to put your faith to the test to *see* if God really will bring you through it? I know you may be reading this book ready to throw it across the room because you think I can't possibly understand where you are right now. That may possibly be true, but God does. God knows exactly where you are. He wants you to ask Him into your mess, right here, right now. Don't skim to the next chapter because you don't want to open yourself up, because this is your moment.

If you want freedom from your chaotic mess, then ask God into your situation. I invite you to say a prayer with me and speak these words into the atmosphere, although they won't mean anything unless you feel them from your heart. But if you truly mean them, they will change your life, forever! Remember, your words have the power of life and death, so let's create some life!

Pray this prayer with me:

> *"Dear Lord, I come to you right now asking for you to forgive me of any sin I may or may not be aware of in my life and allow me to start my communication with you with a clean heart. I thank you for your grace and for your forgiveness. Lord, I can't do this on my own. You know my heart and I'm asking you to take over. I'm putting you in charge of this situation that I'm seeking help with and I am fully trusting that*

*you love me and will do the very best for me. I trust
that you will guide my footsteps and keep me from
stumbling.*

*Thank you for loving me and taking care of my needs.
I know the best thing I can do is trust in you with all
of my heart and not lean on my own understanding.
I'm acknowledging you and I know you will work it
all out for my good. Thank you, Father. Amen."*

After praying that prayer, are you feeling better? Whether you feel
the sensation of instantaneous relief or not, just know that by speaking
those words into the atmosphere, you are changing the course of your
future. You have just given your personal angels something to do
besides sitting on those familiar sidelines, filing their fingernails and
sipping that sweet tea!

BOIL-SCRAPING JOB!

I know you may be saying how it is so much easier to tell someone,
"OK, Honey, trust in the Lord with all your heart and lean not on your
own understanding, in all your ways submit to him, and he will make
your paths straight." (Proverbs 3:5-6). Really, He will?

When you feel as though you are drowning and you can't catch
your breath, it's hard to internalize someone else's King James Version
pick-me-up line. You may as well send me a singing telegram from a
guy dressed in a gorilla costume when I am wallowing in my own mess!

When you are going through something difficult it is challenging to
hear that God has your back while feeling so much pain, even though
deep down you know it. Sometimes it just feels good to wallow and

sing that "woe is me" song. But that doesn't change our situations, does it?

I have felt so many times that God had no clue where I was, and I questioned Him continuously on why He would allow me to suffer with the situation I was facing. I have felt like Job so many times in my life, and I'm sure you have, too.

Poor Job, he was rebuked by his wife who told him to curse God and die. His friends told him that his trials were brought on by his sinful nature. He was covered with boils all over his body. His livestock was destroyed. His children were killed. Everything he had was taken away. I mean, c'mon, who wants to be boil-scraping Job? Not me!

But let's finish the story about Job. Job 42:10-16 says, "After Job had prayed for his friends, the Lord restored his fortunes and gave him twice as much as he had before. All his brothers and sisters and everyone who had known him before came and ate with him in his house. They comforted and consoled him over all the trouble the LORD had brought on him, and each one gave him a piece of silver and a gold ring.

The Lord blessed the latter part of Job's life *more* than the former part. He had fourteen thousand sheep, six thousand camels, a thousand yoke of oxen and a thousand donkeys. And he also had seven sons and three daughters...Nowhere in all the land were there found women as beautiful as Job's daughters...After this, Job lived a hundred and forty years; he saw his children and their children to the fourth generation. And so Job died an old man and full of years."

The lesson here is that when you continue in your trials and keep God first, He *will* bless you for it. He will make Himself so real to you that you won't want to take a step without Him. You will learn that He is greater and mightier than any effort you could possibly conjure up on your own.

Now, if the Lord decides to bless you with thousands of sheep, camels, oxen, and donkeys, you may be called to be a zookeeper. Who knows?

I Finally Found Him...Papa!

Let me show you that God knows exactly where you are, what you need, and how He is ready to make himself known to you and more real than you can possibly imagine.

I was attending a Christian women's retreat where I was expecting to make new friendships and have some major bonding time with the girls. I went expecting to learn new things from the spiritual mothers of the church, and maybe find a little nugget along the way from an anointed guest speaker. All these things were on my checklist to obtain the weekend I went away with 130 women. What I found instead, was what it meant to be a true daughter of the King.

I have heard things my whole life that made me believe God loves me. II Corinthians 6:18 says, "I will be a Father to you, and you will be my sons and daughters, says the Lord Almighty." You hear it in songs: "Jesus Loves Me for the Bible tells me so."

There are literally thousands and thousands of ways the Lord has made himself known to us: in songs, His Word, dreams, and in personal times of struggles. It's endless!

However, even though a person is saved doesn't mean he or she knows what it is to be a daughter/son of God. I think this was a struggle for me because I have the greatest man that ever walked the face of the Earth (besides Jesus himself... ha ha) as my earthly daddy. He has always taken care of me and my needs. He met my every desire. He pampered my sisters and I like we were little princesses. Yes, I am a lucky girl, indeed!

With that being said, I found it hard to place the Creator of the universe on the same platform as my earthly daddy. I mean, c'mon, my daddy changed the broken seal on my toilet when it was leaking. He drove across town to get us a pizza if we were craving it. He took my 2 a.m. phone calls bawling my eyes out because I was having a rough night. He prayed for me. He sat at my bedside when I was a little girl in excruciating pain one night from a three-day-old earache, which by the way completely disappeared after a thirty-second prayer from my faith-filled daddy.

You see, it was hard to place God on that same platform. I didn't know God the same way. I mean, he was *God*. I was not going to ask Him to fix my toilet!

I prayed to God as though He was my genie in a bottle. When I wanted something, I just prayed about it, expecting God to deliver it into my hands.

Did I love God? Absolutely! With everything in me! I invited Him into my day, but to be completely honest, I placed Him on a shelf to watch from a distance. I didn't invite Him into the 2 a.m. phones calls, or the bad day I was having. Not because I didn't want Him there, it just didn't occur to me that He cared about the small things.

My mind always went to this huge, unfathomable entity in the sky. My little pea brain could not come to understand that God was more than the Creator of the Universe. Yes, I knew He loved me. Yes, I knew He cared for me. The Bible lists verse after verse that helped me know that God was for me and not against me.

This takes me to the last night of the women's retreat. The speaker finished up her message and was ready to close out the service. We began singing the song *"Abba, I Belong to You."* Let me just say this song wrecked me. I wasn't listening to how pretty they were singing it, or how off key I was, or watching anyone else in the room. Instead, the Lord drew me into a place of worship that was extremely intimate.

I asked God to make Himself personal and real to me. I began to wonder if my request would be shattered by disappointment or would the Creator of the universe really show up and fulfill it? I didn't want to just see Him as this faceless, invisible entity anymore. I wanted to experience Him in a way I had never experienced Him before.

When I pressed in and continued in my worship, He happily obliged and gave me this vision as I sought him with everything in me: It was extremely bright outside and the grass I was standing on was the greenest grass I had ever seen. Every blade of grass was standing perfectly to make a thick green carpet. In the grass I saw my scuffed up white dress shoes on my little five-year-old feet. Above my shoes were my dingy white dress socks rolled down so perfectly around my ankles. The lace cuff on one of my socks was ripped and a little piece of the lace was hanging over the top of my shoe.

Above that I saw my knobby knees; my left knee had a fresh scab that made the fine blonde hairs on my skinny little legs more prominent. My thin spaghetti-strap sundress had printed pink, white, and yellow flowers and butterflies on it.

My hair was in disarray with my bright blonde pigtails barely touching my shoulders. It looked as though part of my hair was coming loose from each pigtail. On my face was a look of complete and utter innocence with my big, round green eyes appearing to look a little lifeless.

I had a little smudge of dirt on my left cheek that matched the caked dirt underneath my fingernails. My lifeless eyes shifted up and that's when I saw Him. He walked over to me, bent down on His knees, opened up His arms, and said to me, "Lori, I am here with you. I am always here with you. I love that you want to have a more intimate relationship with me because I don't want to just be 'God' to you. You are my beloved daughter and I'm your Papa."

I embraced Papa and melted in His arms. He made Himself real to me and I allowed myself to be vulnerable to accept this perfect gift from Him. He told me when I talk with Him, that I should talk to Him as a child talks to her mommy or daddy. He continued by saying, "Don't just come to me asking me to fix everything and with prayer requests. I want you to just talk to me. Share with me your dreams, your thoughts, your worries, your ambitious goals. You will see that we will go to a deeper place in our relationship. Welcome to this intimate place I have reserved just for you, my beautiful baby girl. Papa loves you!"

With that vision He showed me *how* to be *His little girl.* I didn't have to be perfect. I didn't have to have all the answers. I didn't have to be anything but *His daughter.* He had given me back my innocence and told me he wanted to be invited into my everyday life– that He *wants* to be there.

I invite you to do the same. Allow Him to show you who you *really* are to Him. Not how you see yourself through judgmental eyes, but how beautiful you are on the inside as much as you are on the outside. How much you are valued, adored, accepted, chosen, treasured, cherished, and fought for.

Once you do this, you will view everything differently. You will not pray the same. You won't carry yourself the same. You won't dream the way you used to dream. You will start to dream those big bodacious dreams again and your outlook on things will change.

You may not have that special role model in your life that you can relate to as a daddy or a papa, but that's OK. He is waiting for you to ask Him to fill that role. *You are his child* and He loves you more than you can possibly imagine.

Romans 8:37-39 says this: "No, in all these things we are more than conquerors through Him who loved us. For I am sure that neither death nor life, nor angels nor rulers, nor things present nor things to come, nor powers, nor height nor depth, nor anything else in all creation, will be able to separate us from the love of God in Christ Jesus our Lord." He bottles every tear that you shed...Psalm 56:8. He has the very hairs on your head numbered...Luke 12:7. The Bible is full of verses showing us how He cares for us.

There is nothing that can change His love for you; His word declares it. So that you may know Him more intimately, I invite you to do the following:

1. *Go into your prayer closet and shut the door. If you don't have one already, create one. Create a space that is just for you. Do not take your cell phone, laptop, iPad, iPod, iWatch, tablet, home phone, etc. in there with you.*

2. *Take worship music if that helps you clear your mind.*

3. *Then begin by asking God to reveal the things that might hinder your prayer life. If you have sinned against Him, ask Him to forgive you of those things. If it is unforgiveness against someone, ask Him to show you how to release it.* **Even if you don't feel like forgiving that person, it is imperative to speak that you do, in fact, forgive them.** *This releases Gods power into the situation. I promise the "feeling" of forgiveness will come in time.*

4. *Start thanking Him for your health, even if it isn't perfect. Remember, He is bigger than your problems. Thank Him for your family, yes, even for crazy Uncle Joe. Thank Him for your finances. Thank Him for your home. Thank Him for your employment. Start thanking Him for things He hasn't delivered yet...that's praying in faith, My Dear. Thank Him for whatever comes to your mind. And keep your ears open. He will give you things to be thankful for that you never thought of before.*

5. *Then ask Him to make Himself more real to you than ever before.* **Don't** *give up after 30 seconds when you can't feel the goose bumps popping. Pray it through. This isn't a McDonald's drive- through happy meal, this is shaping your relationship with your Heavenly Father. It may not come in 30 seconds,* **but He will show up!** *I guarantee it!*

Pray this prayer if the words aren't coming to you:

*"**Dear Heavenly Father,** I ask that you bring to my attention anything in my life that is not pleasing to you and forgive my sins. I am coming to you asking for peace of mind and clarity where the enemy is trying to cause confusion. You know me more intimately than anyone else, therefore you know my heart. I'm asking that you reveal yourself to me in a way that I have not yet encountered. Open my eyes and ears to see the wonderful relationship you desire to have with me. Deepen my knowledge of who you are and what role you desire to have in my life. I know you want to be first in my life, and I'm asking you to please place that desire in my heart so that I will place you first. I'm allowing you to have this place in my life and I'm reserving it only for you. Thank you, Lord, for the wonderful gift of you! Amen."*

Are you ready to experience God in a whole new way? I certainly am. Understand that no matter what you do, He still loves you. No matter how much you fail, He still loves you. You can't be separated from His love. You see, good fathers always do what's best for their children. And He is a good, good Father!

STEEL-TOED BOOTS...

When the Lord started the unveiling process of allowing me to see the real Him, the first thing I realized was that it wasn't "I" anymore, it was *all Him*! After fighting every demon in Hell to get to this unveiling process, the Lord began to finally open my eyes to see my new territory of ministry. And let me tell ya, it was a little scary! Actually, it was *very* scary!

My territory included opening my home to host a ladies' Bible study. It included the most remote locations in Uganda Africa. It included the most poverty-stricken areas in Columbus, Ohio. And your territory will include places you never thought possible.

I am a completely different person than when I started this journey with the Lord. I was a person who felt extremely humbled that the Lord found me worthy to try my faith and to show me who He really is. I started looking at things differently. For the first time I looked at things not as a victim, but as a person who could do something for the Kingdom of God.

For the first time *ever* in my life I didn't want to say, "*I* quit smoking. *I* quit drinking. Look what *I* did." Instead I wanted to say, "Look what the Lord did for me!" I wanted to see how big He could get. I think I kept the Lord in a small box for so long because I was afraid of disappointment yet again. If I prayed for something and it didn't happen, that meant my faith wasn't strong enough, right? Wrong. It means it hasn't happened *yet*.

I looked at my relationship with Him as, "God is in Heaven, I love Him, and I want to make it to Heaven one day." That's it. But after the unveiling started, wow! He got bigger and bigger, and I got more and more excited wondering how much bigger He could possibly get. Let me tell you, friends, He is to this day still amazing me at how big He is!

My whole point in sharing with you all the details of my past and the sins I have committed, every wrong decision, bad luck, twist of fate, whatever you want to label it, is because *I have been there!* If it could happen, I have probably experienced it. I have just about seen it all, done it all, witnessed it all, smelled it all, felt it all, numbed out to feeling it all, lied about it, snuck around about it, covered it up, etc... You name it; I undoubtedly have been in the same room with it!

I used to be naïve enough to think I was the only one in the world with problems this big. I mean, come on. Give me a break. My problems were so much worse than Anna's and uglier than Rachel's. My addictions were stronger than Aly's. My hatred toward men was by far worse than Ashley's. My finances were more out of control than Tina's. My self-image was more lacking than Caitlyn's. My previous relationships were more chaotic than Sonia's. My depression was darker than Misty's. I always felt that I was far worse off than I probably was, and that somehow my problems are what shaped me into the person I am today and that I had to be defined by my circumstances.

Wow, when this hit me, I honestly felt like a ton of bricks hit me on my ignorant little head! How highly did I really regard myself anyway, that my problems and the things I went through were so much worse than anyone else's? That's when I heard that familiar little voice in my head say clear as day, "It's not about you, it's about Me." What? "Of course, it's about me; I'm the one you are trying to fix, Lord. I am the rape victim. I am the victim of drug addiction and alcoholism. I am the victim of horrible finances. I am the victim of depression. I am the victim, Lord." Of course, I said all these things in my most girlish, please feel sorry for me voice! Then the Lord absolutely blew me away and said, "No Lori, *I AM!*"

Talk about bringing someone down a few notches in a hurry! I was absolutely blown away and couldn't even think for the next several hours. What in the world just happened? Did the Lord really just step on my toes? Was I really rebuked by the King of Kings! I knew I should have worn my steel-toed boots today!

Did I actually have the audacity to complain to the Lord about being a victim and want sympathy for the horrible things that had happened to me? Wasn't that carrying around the "victim hat" and wearing it when it was convenient? How in the world could the Lord heal all those hurts if I was still complaining and carrying around the handicap label of "victim"?

I thought about that for a long while. I wasn't able to shake the daunting words He'd spoken: *I am.* It seemed the more I tried to figure out what the Lord meant by those few words He'd spoken to me, the more I felt ashamed of my victim mentality. So I began to ask God, "What do you want to reveal to me? Lord, I'll get rid of the 'victim hat' and stop the 'I ams' if you show me what you meant when you said '*I am.*"

Over the next several months He began lifting the veil so I could see clearer. This was a whole new world for me; (yes, I'm singing "A Whole New World" as sung in the movie *Aladdin!* Ha ha...) it was a world in which I didn't play the victim anymore. A world that seemed so much brighter than the one I had been residing in. For some strange reason I began to have hope that life was about to get really, really good.

God had given me a clear picture of what I was in search of. I got *me* out of the way and finally allowed the Lord to take the front seat. It was all about Him. What seems so clear cut and simple right here in black and white was an extremely difficult task for me because I wasn't the one in control anymore. But I finally gave the keys over to Him and allowed Him to drive. Let me tell ya, I never knew being a passenger could be so freeing. I put my feet up on the dashboard, I cranked up the radio, rolled the windows down and let the sunshine hit my face. I trusted the Lord to take me anywhere. It's as if I could see Him hand me a pair of sunglasses as he told me to sit back, relax, and enjoy the ride!

IT'S YOUR TIME...

He is ready to start the unveiling process with you, too. Are you ready? I believe you are. I believe the unveiling process has already begun, the seeds have been planted and it's time for the Lord to make Himself more real than ever before to you. This is your time.

It's not about me, it's about you. It is why God prompted you to read this book. It's not just a story of a woman who had a rough life, made bad decisions, and took the wrong road. It is all about a person God chose to do a work in: you.

For anyone who is looking for hope, it is here. For anyone who has prayed for love to return to his or her marriage, it is here. For anyone who has beckoned the Lord to do a miracle in himself or herself or a family member, it is here. For anyone that has prayed endlessly for salvation for his or her children, it is here. For anyone who has been told she couldn't succeed, it is here. For anyone who is fighting an addiction, it is here. For anyone who is looking for the answers about why you don't feel the need to be completely honest with your spouse, it is here. For anyone who holds his emotions deep inside, fearful of sharing completely, it is here. For anyone with the spirit of suicide, it is here. For anyone who wants to feel like the family provider again, it is here. For anyone who wants her children to look at her like she is a hero, it is here. For anyone who wants to be the person God created him or her to be, it is here. The answers lie straight ahead.

Enough about the rough road I traveled, let's travel down the road that gives you the keys to true, undying, unconditional love and freedom. Let's get the answers about how to get out of the victim role and into the victor role; the answers are here!

So, I am going to challenge you. I challenge you to take off the victim hat, remove the sunglasses, open up those beautiful eyes of yours and visit a world that has been waiting for you. This is one time that the Lord asks you to get out of the boat and get wet! Dive in! The water is fine!

~ Another link has been broken ~

CHAPTER 6
OUT OF HIDING

D ID YOU KNOW that uncovering the Devil's schemes can remove the shadows and darkness that he works in? Once things are brought out of hiding, you have officially stripped him of his power. Are you hiding an old, unhealthy habit from your pre-Jesus days that is holding you back from walking in complete freedom? Did you know that once you uncover what the enemy wants to keep hidden, then God can start His restoration process with you? Let's look at what uncovering the enemy's tactics can do for you.

I am going to be completely transparent here, I thought that being saved and going to church was enough to keep the boogeyman away... it's not.

In the next few chapters, we are going to talk about how we as Christians can walk in complete freedom by uncovering the Devil's hidden agenda and what that looks like for each one of us. I'm going to explain why the Devil wants us to be ignorant to these facts and how we get from living in bondage to walking in complete freedom. These are the exact questions that I answered for myself when the Lord showed me that Christianity was more than attending church once a week, it was a relationship with Abba Father.

I, like many people, was deceived by thinking that just because God was in my heart that the Devil didn't occasionally have my ear. And to be honest, having my heart dedicated to Jesus but lending my ears to the Devil is a definite way to live in complete confusion and chaos, and that is *not* what the Lord wants for our lives.

I wanted more than anything to be free of the emotional baggage I had carried around, but the enemy masked his existence in my life just as soon I would start to uncover his ploys. This was an exhausting way to live. We touched a little bit on how to get rid of the emotional baggage we carry around a few chapters back, but I would like to dive in a little deeper.

The Lord revealed to me one night at a prayer meeting that I had unknowingly allowed the Devil to continue his antics because I had not uncovered the hidden sins in my life: bitterness, pride, victim mentality, anger and rage. This was not a fun realization to have.

I couldn't quite comprehend this concept because I was a saved, sanctified Christian of several years and was trying to live right. But I was walking around in so much confusion because the Devil masked his existence in ways that made me think that *his* thoughts were actually *my* thoughts. The Devil then made me think that this was a normal and acceptable way to live. Boy oh boy, he is such a deceiver!

I was deceived into thinking that these spirits were my personality traits and not the enemy's ploy to continue robbing me of my complete freedom. I had carried them around so long that I didn't even realize they had become who I was and how I identified myself.

Then the Lord revealed to me that it was time to uncover the enemy and shine a light on what the Devil had tried to keep hidden. He showed me that I had made friends with bitterness, pride, victim mentality, anger, and rage, just to list a few, and it was time to take back what the enemy had stolen from me.

We will look at what has been hidden in your life and how we uncover what the Devil is *terrified* of you finding out. God called us to live in freedom, so let's take the necessary steps to take back what the enemy has stolen from us.

The Big Ten...

Can you tell me the first thing that comes to mind when you hear the words "The Big Ten?" You may have said football, and if you did that's not quite what I was talking about, but that's OK. OH-IO. See, I can enjoy a little sports humor, too.

Actually, I'm talking about the Ten Commandments. Let me ask you, do you feel the Ten Commandments are enslaving you? Do you feel that they are a bunch of rules to you or do you feel that they are a pedestal for true freedom?

The fact that God would manifest ten specific commandments shows how important they are. I personally believe He gave them as a guideline for us so we could walk in true freedom!

Exodus 20:2 says, "I am the Lord your God, who brought you out of Egypt, out of the land of slavery." He then proceeds to list the Ten Commandments:

1. *You shall have no other gods before me.*

2. *You shall not make for yourself an idol.*

3. *You shall not misuse the name of the Lord your God.*

4. *Remember the Sabbath day by keeping it holy.*

5. *Honor your father and your mother.*

6. *You shall not murder.*

7. *You shall not commit adultery.*

8. *You shall not steal.*

9. *You shall not give false testimony against your neighbor.*

10. *You shall not covet.*

Wikipedia gives the definition of slavery as this:

> *"Slavery is a legal system in which principles of property are applied to humans allowing them to be classified as property; they are owned, bought, and sold and they cannot withdraw from the arrangement. While a person is a slave, the owner is entitled to the productivity of the slave's labor."*

But if God's word says that we are no longer slaves, then why do we tend to keep ourselves in bondage to a lifestyle that is no longer designed for us?

Understanding this is a key element to breaking free and to walking completely in what God has in store for you.

I believe it is because of all those little enslaving demons that creep back in with different faces. You throw one off of you and boom, there is another one there to take its place. It's sad that we have grown accustomed to living like this and we don't even recognize it.

The Devil will try and oppress what threatens him! The enemy is very deceiving. He knows once you recognize him, he's doomed. That's why he always changes the face of the battle. The enemy has thousands of faces to disguise himself. It's not just a high school term; he truly is two-faced!

The Devil tries to parade around unseen. That's why he masquerades around *silently* with names such as self-pity, doubt, fear, anger, bitterness, resentment, procrastination, laziness, shame, busyness, worry, anxiety, panic, gossip, unfriendliness, pride, conceit, low self-esteem, lack of self-respect…the list is endless. These are some of the names that the enemy uses to mask his identity. He is lying to us saying that these spirits are just personality traits. That is a lie from the pits of Hell!

You may identify with at least one of these, or if you are like me, you can identify with *most* of them. And I did say identify, *not* claim or

98

label yourself with them. These tend to be "silent" because they creep in without us even knowing it. Once the enemy has a foothold it gives him leverage to work. If the Devil can gain access to you, guess what, he brings many friends with him. Before you know it, you are in the midst of an all-out war! Those little voices in your head become what you hear about yourself daily! He makes people a slave to his lies!

We must guard our hearts and our minds constantly. That's why the Bible says in Romans 12:2, "Do not conform to the pattern of this world but be transformed by the renewing of your mind."

This is the beginning of true freedom: recognize what has your attention, your thought process, and your mind. Once you have identified how the enemy is masquerading around you, it's time to evict him! I'm talking about doing it with *big bold bodacious prayers* and uncovering him completely!

Once we uncover what he wants us to keep hidden, he knows the game is over. And we just cannot afford to allow him to have control over us any longer!

Poop-Covered Fleas!

Let's take a look at what uncovering the enemy's schemes can do in our lives. The following is a story about a dear friend of mine who stopped the Devil dead in his tracks and what happened when he was exposed.

My friend, I will call her Jessica, was a saved Christian and had been serving the Lord for a few years when she asked my opinion about what she should do in relation to quitting a "habit from her past...her pre-Jesus days."

Have I told you that I absolutely love giving my opinion and telling people what to do? Most people call this being bossy and controlling. I call it great leadership skills.

I was completely humbled that she would make herself vulnerable enough to share this with me, knowing I could have been completely judgmental about her situation. But instead of judging her, I explained that it was not my role to pass judgment. My role was to guide her to see what God had to say about her situation.

Jessica wanted to know what I thought about her quitting this "thing" because she wasn't sold on the idea of having to give it up completely. She felt that it was OK to do it and was trying to rationalize it in her own mind.

However, she was beginning to feel that it was wrong and felt guilty about it, which led to our conversation. This was even more tormenting to her because now she was smack dab in the middle of an all-out spiritual war. Her thoughts were something like this: *Do I quit? Do I continue? Do I quit? Do I continue? Do I quit? Do I continue?* I'm sure you can relate to this back-and-forth tug of war that she was experiencing.

God was trying to draw her closer to Him while the enemy was having a heyday keeping the chaos and confusion going. The Devil was lying to her telling her that it was OK to continue doing that one thing from the past and to keep it hidden.

The Devil knew how to keep that door cracked open so that he could have full access anytime he wanted it. He wanted to be able to crawl back in anytime he wanted so he could wreak havoc in her life. Isn't it just like that slimy little sucker? He will sugarcoat a poop-covered flea and tell you it tastes delicious! So be careful and watch what the enemy tries to get you to eat! Remember, he is a liar!

Jessica stated that she didn't even know who she was anymore after giving her life to the Lord. It was a life she had always wanted but she couldn't help but feel a little bit of grief seeing her old lifestyle chiseled away right before her very own eyes.

She felt she had given up everything. She didn't hang out at the bars or drink alcohol anymore. She no longer hosted parties at her house. Her group of friends had changed. Who she hung around with changed. What she watched on TV changed. The way she communicated with people changed. But this one little thing from the past she couldn't quite give up. It had dug in deep and was holding on for dear life.

I'm sure she thought to herself she should have just kept it a secret and dealt with the situation by herself, hoping the voice of conviction would go away eventually.

Sometimes we feel that our sin is better in the dark where no one will see it! And that is *exactly* where the Devil wants us to keep it. He would love nothing more than for us to keep our dirty little secrets hidden and out of sight. Because in the darkness things are covered and not exposed. *That's the key to the enemy's power: keeping things hidden!*

Keeping things hidden will only lead you down a road where disaster meets catastrophe. Before long, our one hidden sin turns into shame and guilt we feel from hiding it. Then it turns into lying. Lying turns into pride. Pride turns into a hardened heart. Do you see where I'm going with this?

When we feel shame, guilt, and pride what does that do? It starts turning us away from God. I mean, let's face it, who wants to have an intimate relationship with God, the Master of the Universe, with a bag full of yuck? I'll tell ya who: no one. This can soon become a slow fade away from our relationship with Him if we are not careful.

The enemy knows our triggers and exploits them. Rarely will you see the enemy go up to someone, hand him a gun, and tell him to go kill someone. That type of craziness is so bold and flamboyant that pretty much anyone can see the enemy working there and will run in the opposite direction like his hair is on fire.

As in Song of Solomon 2:15, it says, the little foxes that spoil the vine. When the enemy comes at us so sneaky stating words you can easily mistake as your own, it's easier to sit and eat dinner with him. It's the Devil saying, "C'mon, you deserve this one last vice from your past. It's not hurting anyone. No one even knows about it. Don't tell anyone. They will think you're weak and a hypocrite of a Christian." Are these voices plaguing your mind? Do they sound familiar? Do you hear the enemy telling you these same little lies? If so, it's time to grab a bullhorn and shout SHUT UP to the Devil!

The question at hand is this: Is it hurting someone even if no one knows about it? The answer is yes, it is hurting you. And it was hurting Jessica, too.

Are you thinking the same thing I was thinking? What in the world does Jessica possess that the Devil was terrified of seeing her completely free? I'll tell you what she possessed: she possessed the light of the one true living God and the Devil did not want her blinders to come off so that *she* could see who she really was in Him!

But the enemy would not stop taunting her. He wanted to keep the door open to the past. If he could keep her blind to his attack, he would win. And let's face it, no one wants the boogeyman to win!

After she asked my opinion on this matter, I prayed and told her what I felt the Lord wanted me to say.

I suggested that she "fast" that item, meaning she should abstain from it for a period of time that she decided on with the Lord. And while she fasted that item, she should be in prayer about what the Lord wanted her to do about it.

I knew the Lord wanted her to finally be able to walk in the full extent of her calling, but she had to completely and totally submit to what He wanted for her. Once she decided to abstain from that item, the situation got even worse. I know this doesn't sound like a happily ever after story, but bear with me, you will see that God serves the enemy a poop-covered flea to eat.

The enemy was coming at her in every direction. He was lying to her telling her she wasn't going to be the same person anymore. She started feeling overwhelmed and anxious. She felt her entire identity was being swept away. When in all reality she was shedding that old skin off and allowing God to form her the way He saw her.

When she finally made up her mind that there was no turning back, and she called the Devil to the carpet, the voices stopped. When she sacrificed what she felt she had a right to do for the sake of getting closer to the Lord, God stepped in and shut the mouth of the enemy for her! I told you this was going to get good!

There are times when God will allow you to be pushed to the limit to see how much *you* are willing to take from the Devil. Of course, God can step in anytime He wants to and knock the teeth out of the enemy. I mean, c'mon, He's God. But He wants you to see how much you will take from the enemy before saying enough is enough!

Jessica said she felt like a weak person for feeling the way she did, but in all reality, she had the strength of Sampson. It takes a lot for a person to expose her flaws and secrets, but this is what ultimately set her completely free. She pulled everything out of the dark and out of hiding and allowed the Lord to fling it into Hell where it came from.

FIGHT LIKE YOU ARE THE THIRD TIGER ON NOAH'S ARK!

When you can do this for yourself and bring things out of hiding into the light then you will see who you are in God and what you contain. By doing this, you strip the enemy of his power over you.

There are no more secrets. There is no more shame. There are no more lies. There is nothing the enemy can do to you now! You have, in all reality, won your life back!

The Devil is so sneaky at blackmailing people and making them afraid of revealing the truth. When something is brought out of hiding that means something is found. When we get to the point when we tell the enemy we are not going to be in bondage to his lies any longer, or that we are not keeping "our secret" hidden anymore, that's when we gain our power and freedom.

We basically take the demonic spirits of guilt, shame, fear, pride—you name it—and tell them they have *no more* power over us. When they are exposed, they can't torment you any longer.

So my question is this, are you going to continue taking what the Devil dishes out, or are you going to stand up and say enough is enough, I'm not hiding anymore?

I trust that the Lord has stirred something up inside of you and it's time to come out of hiding. It's time to uncover what the enemy has kept in darkness all this time. Whether it is hidden credit card debt you have kept from your spouse, a secret drinking problem, a mental disorder you deal with, a drug addiction, pornography, sexual confusion, an eating disorder, anger issues, lust, being a workaholic, domestic violence, technology addiction, lying, stealing, or laziness. Whatever it is that you deal with, God can heal it once He is put in charge of it.

Your first step is to acknowledge what your hidden sin(s) are. The second step is to bring it before the Lord keeping nothing secret. He's not a mean, judging God. He's a loving Father who wants you to be free, just like you would want your own child to be free. Once you bring it out of hiding, and submit completely to the Lord, He can start the healing process with whatever you put Him in charge of.

Now is the time to put yourself in a timeout and pray like you have never prayed before. Don't pray meek and timid prayers. Instead, pray as you feel the fire in your belly rise up. You may even feel a spiritual anger escalate; it's OK to feel this. That's when you demand that every demon in Hell flee in the name of Jesus! Call out every name you can think of that you deal with and rebuke it in the name of Jesus. If you deal with anger, then call out anger! If it's bitterness, then call out bitterness! If it's greed, call it out! If it's laziness, call it out! If it's fear, call it out!

Now is the time to identify your demons and step into your own personal boxing ring and fight! Fight like there is no tomorrow. When you start identifying what you wish to expel from your life, then God can step in and act on your words. Remember the scripture in Proverbs 18:21, "Death and life are in the power of the tongue..."

We need to learn to speak life over ourselves and our circumstances. I invite you to pray this prayer with me:

"Dear Heavenly Father, I come to you asking to speak to the Lion of Judah, my fighting warrior. I'm asking that you take me by the hand and go with me to the battle line. As you gave David the courage, faith, and strength to slay Goliath, I'm asking that you help me slay my giants. Every putrid and disgusting demon that has had my attention up to this point now has to flee in the name of Jesus. Satan, I am hand in hand with God to evict you! You no longer have my permission to be here and you must go. You are no longer welcome here. I'm taking my life back and cleaning house. Devil, you will not define me anymore and I will no longer be a home for you and your imps! This minute I am declaring war on you! You ...are...evicted! Thank you, Father, for your son's name, Jesus. Because of that name, I am free–truly free. Amen."

In this prayer time with God, He may show you that there are times to be in war mode and to be spiritually angry. Sometimes you will have to take Hell like Jesus did and run toward the line that has been drawn in the sand by the enemy and cross it...and not just cross it but declare *war* and take it by force!

I saw this on a meme the other day and couldn't help but giggle a little bit. It said, "If you're gonna fight, fight like you're the third tiger on the ramp to Noah's Ark...and sister, it's starting to rain!" I love that. Now is not the time to pray pretty prayers, people. It's time to tap into your fierce side and take back what the enemy has stolen from you!

SHUT UP, DEVIL!

Once you have uncovered and brought out of darkness what has held you in your own prison all this time, it's time to see what the Lord has said about you walking in freedom and taking your life back.

Let's keep in mind that the enemy's job is to lie to you and tell you that you will never be free. That's his first line of defense, and it's a lie. Then he will try and consume your mind with doubt and intimidation. He will whisper in your ear that your secret or secrets are just too big to overcome; that's another lie. He will tell you that the people in your life will think badly of you and view you differently once they know your secret or what you have been hiding; again, another lie.

Are those voices already plaguing your mind? If they are, tell the enemy to *shut up!* He wants to cloud your mind so you can't think straight; this is his defense. If he can keep you freaked out and scared to the point of not taking action, he wins. Do *not* let him win!

My mom never allowed us to say "shut up" growing up because she thought it was rude. Well, this is one time I think it's OK to say it, and I think my mom would agree. Shut up! Shut up! Shut up, Devil!

The Bible says in II Corinthians 10:5 "We demolish arguments and every pretension that sets itself up against the knowledge of God, and we take captive every thought to make it obedient to Christ." We have the power to make our thoughts obedient! How awesome is that! So, when those thoughts come to mind that the enemy places there, you have the power, through Christ, to cast them down. We do not have to entertain the Devil's lies any longer. When something enters your mind that doesn't produce life, it's as simple as saying, "nope, not going to entertain that thought...Devil, you gotta go!"

And the Word of God says that whoever the Son sets free, is free indeed! This is God's word. When we speak and stand on his word, no Devil in Hell can stand against it. This promise of God's is enough to make me want to run around my house and dance and shout and stomp on the Devils head! What about you? Are you ready to do a little dance on the Devils head?

I'm going to ask you to pray about your situation. Ask God what you should do with what you have uncovered and exposed. He may tell you that exposing it to Him is enough. He may ask you to reveal it to someone else in confidence. He may ask that you bring it to someone and ask that person for forgiveness. This process is entirely up to the Lord. But trust that whatever He asks you to do, He already has your road mapped out and ready for your journey.

Keep in mind that the Lord is not going to ask you to do something that will rip your life apart. That's another lie from the enemy. He's doing the opposite - He is cleaning out those old cobwebs in your spirit that have kept things hidden for way too long. He's giving you your power back. How awesome is that? This will take faith to walk in, but like the scripture says in Matthew 17:20, He replied, "Because you have so little faith. Truly I tell you, if you have faith as small as a mustard seed, you can say to this mountain, 'Move from here to there,' and it will move. Nothing will be impossible for you."

This will be a process you and the Lord will go through together. Remember to spend some quality quiet time with Him so you can hear what He is leading you to do. This process may be difficult, but trust in it. This is where the picture of *you* starts becoming crystal clear. This is where you can feel confident holding that mirror in your hand and to ask the question, "Mirror, mirror on the wall, who's the fairest of them all?" And I guarantee the Lord will whisper in your ear, "My Dear, you are."

LEMON-SCENTED PLEDGE...

Once you have started to spiritually clean house, you may realize that some of Satan's imps are fighting for dear life to hold on to the residence that has become their home for many years, maybe even decades. But when you stand on God's word and walk in faith that you are truly free, your very words are what divides and conquers things in the spiritual realm.

When I was a kid it was routine for my sisters and I to clean house every Saturday. Our Saturday cleaning consisted of what most people call spring or fall cleaning. People usually do this type of cleaning a few times a year...not in my mama's house. Now keep in mind that my mom had three teenage daughters with an endless flow of neighborhood kids through our home. Our house was the neighborhood hangout. My mom wanted to keep an eye on us and what we were up to and what better way to do that than invite the entire neighborhood to hang out at our house. Smart mama!

So, we would wash baseboards. Wipe walls down. Laundry cleaned, folded, and put away. We swept under beds. Everything had to be picked up and moved to dust. We mopped and swept the floors. Wiped down the banisters. This was a few of the chores we did on Saturdays. All of this took place while the Statler Brothers belted out their tunes from our 700-pound TV console/record player. When we cleaned, we cleaned with lemon-scented Pledge. That's when you knew it was "Saturday cleaned."

It's funny to see how my twin sister Lisa hates the smell of lemons and I absolutely love it. When I burn those lemon cubes in my Scentsy burner at my house and she walks in, she says, "It smells like Mom's house growing up." But that is when you knew the house was *completely* clean.

When God sets us free from what has imprisoned us, just know, my dear, that you are going to smell lemons! He doesn't do it halfway or tease you with a little bit of freedom here and there. This is complete spiritual freedom.

Keep in mind that having something and walking in it can be two different things. You can own the most beautiful diamond bracelet. Keep it in the plush bag it came in. Take out an insurance policy on it in case something happens to it. But if you don't put it on and wear it what good it is sitting in that velvet bag somewhere?

God can set you free, but you can get up, walk away, and pick up the very thing God delivered you from. *Don't do that.* Do not allow the enemy to confuse you on this. This is why it's good to find what God's word says about it and stand on it! Here are just a few:

- *Galatians 5:1 says, "It is for freedom that Christ has set us free. Stand firm then, and do not let yourselves be burdened again by a yoke of slavery."*

- *Luke 4:18 says, ."..He has sent me to proclaim freedom for the prisoner and recovery of sight for the blind, to set the oppressed free."*

- *II Corinthians 3:17 says, "Now the Lord is the Spirit, and where the Spirit of the Lord is, there is Freedom."*

You can take these scriptures and post them throughout your home and when the enemy comes at you, you have already posted the Word. It's your own personal "Keep Out" sign. Just recite your scriptures and watch him run away. After a while, he will see he has no access to gain entry and he will leave you alone. It does not mean he won't come back occasionally, looking for a way in, but you will have the keys, in hand, ready to use them as a sword to poke his eyes out! Instead of the enemy blinding you, turn the tables and blindside him!

GIANT KILLER!

There are key elements in spiritual warfare that the Lord has set out before us in His word. So let's take a look at the example of what David did.

When David went toward the battle line to fight Goliath, it says he ran quickly toward Goliath (1 Samuel 17:48). Why do you suppose that is? If you were ready to fight a giant, do you think you would run toward the battle line or tuck tail and run in the opposite direction? I have to be honest and say I would have probably faked an injury of some sort and run like the wind far away from that giant!

But I think one of the reasons David ran quickly is because if he didn't, it's quite possible that it may have given Goliath a chance at an early attack. But David was prepared and ready for battle. David fought, he won, game over. But David had another purpose in life; it was to be king. Isn't it weird how we sometimes tend to go to the David and Goliath story rather than the King David story?

As much as I love that story (it truly is one of my favorites, mainly because I am a born fighter and it resonates with my spirit), I truly believe God wanted David's legacy to be as King David. A little shepherd boy turns giant killer, later to become king. What's not to love about that story?

But sometimes we seem to highlight and focus on the battle more than the victory. Why is it that our war wounds seem so much more fascinating than our victories? Why do we focus more on our "Goliaths" than the "kingships" God is calling us to? I believe it's because the enemy has had us on the defense for so long instead of us playing the offense. We have spent too much time fighting for our lives rather than resting at His feet. We will explore this more in Chapter 8.

Killing Goliath was not God's main objective for David. Fighting day in and day out just to keep your head above water is not what God wants you to do. If we are constantly in war mode, then we can't be in worship mode with the Father.

Now, let me say that I truly believe it *is* absolutely necessary to take the head off of our enemy when it arises, but that's the key: taking the head off—not pacifying it, not tolerating it, and not making friends with it. There's nothing worse than making friends with the demonic spirits the enemy has plagued us with. We can't walk in the fullness of God if we have made "frenemies" (a person with whom one is friendly despite a fundamental dislike or rivalry…you know, someone you love to hate) with them.

When David decided to walk out and face Goliath, what do you think he was feeling? Well, from a carnal standpoint, I think he may have felt rejected and not good enough to complete the task at hand. Why? Because three times by three different people (his brother Eliab, King Saul, and Goliath) he was told he was too small and puny. He was youthful, ruddy, and handsome. He was laughed at for what he brought to fight with, his sling shot, which was the very thing that slayed this giant!

You see, it's *what* you carry that will slay your giant. David refused to buy into others' opinions of him. He only listened to the voice of his

Father and the Father said to *fight!*

Once you figure out what God is saying to you, that's where freedom comes in. Freedom in Christ is simple: it is choosing to believe God at His word and walking in it!

There comes a time when we want to see how big God is and find out what it means to have true peace. Not the kind of peace that disappears at the first sign of trouble, but true, lasting peace.

I made a New Year's resolution years ago. It wasn't about exercising more. It wasn't about being nicer or being a more giving person. It wasn't even about being a better mom. Of course, those things seemed like obvious choices to be on my list, but the choice I made was this: to find the true meaning of peace.

It's not how little or how much you pray, and it's not about how many books you have read on the topic. He revealed to me that true peace comes from inside. It is realizing that no matter what circumstance you are facing, He will never leave you nor forsake you. It's knowing that if you are going through it, He allowed it to strengthen you or to teach you. It is knowing that you're not a failure because you haven't completed some checklist that you created in hopes of becoming a happier person.

True peace is knowing it's not a personality trait or a tangible thing to obtain; it's an ongoing process each and every day. And depending on the day, it comes easily or it's something you rip out of the jaws of the enemy because it's yours!

The Lord searched my heart and revealed this to me: It's not how many badges of honor you carry on your sleeve due to the many trials you have managed to crawl out of. It's carrying God with you in every situation and allowing Him to be part of your mindset, your thoughts, your encouragement, your heart, your wisdom, and your knowledge. That's the key to true peace.

There is an old saying that goes like this: You begin to act like those you surround yourself with. So if you are walking with the Prince of Peace, how can you not have a little bit of peace rub off on you?

Obtaining true peace is resolving in your mind that no matter what circumstance comes your way, you choose to believe that God loves you and has everything under control...*no matter what.*

How Dead is Dead?

Take the story of Lazarus in the book of Luke. Lazarus is dead for four days when Jesus shows up. Now, that's about as final as a situation gets, right? But Jesus didn't run to the tomb crying and freaking out over the death of His friend. He displayed true peace over the situation by thanking God for hearing him and then calling Lazarus out. His words demanded that death release its hold on Lazarus. You see, peace comes when there is confidence in knowing who you belong to; that's the key to peace. He had confidence in what he did because he was in constant communication with the Father.

When we focus on who we belong to instead of our circumstances, peace is there. The moment we realize our identity in Christ, we will walk in a level of power and authority that no Devil can combat!

When we really understand the love of God and how much He loves each and every one of us, it's easy to rest in the fact that He wants the best for us. He will withhold nothing good from us. That's where peace comes from.

I know you are saying to yourself, "Yeah, well, that was Jesus. Of course He has true peace." Well, the same Spirit of God that is in Jesus also lives in you if you are a born-again Christian.

John 14:12 says, "I tell you the truth, anyone who believes in me will do the same works I have done, *and even greater works,* because I am going to be with the Father." Jesus already foretold that we would be able to do greater things than He did. So let's start claiming victory over our situations. Once we do, peace will surely follow.

We can't pick apart the Bible and only believe certain parts of it. We either believe what He said or we don't. I don't know about you, but I want to have so much God in me that the very residue that rolls off of me gives the guy standing behind me in the grocery line a Holy Ghost fit!

So as you have uncovered the hidden agenda from the enemy in your situation and have exposed him, it's time to move to the next step and discover what the uncovered, surrendered you looks like.

You will see that walking in this newfound freedom is where God intended us all to be.

I invite you to say this prayer with me;

"Dear Heavenly Father, I want to thank you for shining your light on the hidden dangers and hidden areas in my life that the enemy has tried to keep concealed. I am so appreciative that you have walked me through this process. You have shown me how revealing these things allows me to walk in complete freedom and I am trusting that you will fill those empty places in me with your spirit. I'm grateful that you have shown me that I have complete authority over the enemy. Lord, I am excited to see what this next chapter in our relationship looks like. In Jesus's name, Amen."

~ Another link has been broken ~

CHAPTER 7
WHO'S YOUR DADDY?

As we move forward into this next chapter, we will look at what our new identity in Christ looks like after we have uncovered the hidden pitfalls from the Devil. We will discover how walking in your new identity sets you up for a newfound freedom God wants for each one of us.

I titled this chapter "Who's Your Daddy" so we could journey together and see what God has to say about who you are in Him. Once we start seeing ourselves through the eyes of God instead of our own jaded views, our identity will shift into God's reality, not our own.

"Who's Your Daddy?" is a tag line in a few movies. It's been used in video games and even in the sports arena as sporting teams try and one up each other. It is a theme of a reality daytime TV show in which individuals try and figure out the paternity of their children. It is also the title of a hit song from Toby Keith. But there came a time when those three little words consumed my thoughts and I couldn't escape them.

It came from hearing story after story of people like you and me who didn't truly know who they were or what their purpose in life was. It came from a lack of identity. This was mind boggling to me. I couldn't fathom the idea that Christians who are born again, sanctified, and serving God with everything in them didn't have any idea of who they were or what their true purpose was.

You see, you can wake up and live life every day without really stepping into your God-given calling and that is where a person's true identity comes from. You can have an identity the world places on you or you can have the identity of who God says you are.

Beware my friend, the world is a very unkind and unjust place to get your stats from; you see, the world is going to lie to you. It will tell you that you must be a certain weight to be pretty. It will tell you that you have to drive a certain car to be cool. Is "cool" even a cool word anymore? The world will tell you that you have to get a certain college degree to really matter in the workplace. The world is going to tell you that your children have to be involved in thirteen different activities to be considered well-rounded. The world is going to tell you that you have to work a full-time job *and* be a full-time parent at home and balance it beautifully. The world is going to tell you that you always have to have X-amount of money in the bank with a huge 401K and a separate retirement plan to be considered financially stable. The world is going to tell you that pride, money, finances, and activities are where your identity is. I'm here to tell you, they are not.

With that being said, I am not going to say that there isn't some value in some of the things I just listed, *but* within reason, and keep in mind that they do *not* make up your identity. The *things* in life shouldn't make up your identity—they should only enhance the true you.

If you base your identity on these things, what happens when the world throws you a curveball and you gain twenty pounds? Or your car dies, and you can't afford another one because you haven't paid off the one that just died? Or your children decide they don't want to participate in the activities you signed them up for because they want to experience being a kid instead of being a slave to society's perception of what makes a well-rounded child? What happens when you lose your job and all the wealth you managed to stash away has now disappeared because you used it to survive? What happens when depression or anxiety has taken over your life and you can't manage to make it through the long dreadful day anymore?

I'll tell you what happens, you place your identity in who God says you are and watch things start to shift. And when the veil starts to lift, you can probably bet that the enemy is going to be right there tempting you the same way he tempted Jesus, in His identity!

In Luke 4:3 it says, "The Devil said to him, *'If you are the Son of God, tell this stone to become bread.'*" Is the Devil really trying to take a stab at the identity of Jesus? You see, if the Devil wouldn't leave the Son of God's identity alone, he sure isn't going to leave you alone.

But look at what Jesus's response was, and keep in mind Jesus is showing us how to respond in situations like this. He said in Matthew 4:4, *"It is written: 'Man shall not live on bread alone but by every word that proceeds out of the mouth of God.'"* And when did the Devil tempt Jesus? *After* he had fasted for 40 days, when he was the hungriest! Don't allow yourself to become so hungry that you will just gorge on anything.

You see, the Devil didn't come to Jesus tempting him right after he ate a large beautiful meal and his belly was full. He waited until just the right time to strike, when it seemed the hardest to refuse him. But even in the most trying times, God's word is sharp enough to shut the mouth of the enemy. You just have to speak it and stand on it.

The enemy will try and keep you bound and confused in this area because he knows that once you see your *true* self and that you have the weapons of Heaven on your side, his lies don't mean anything anymore. Take a minute and let this marinate with you.

Of course we are all going to face struggles in life. The Bible even says in 1 Peter 4:12-13, "Beloved, think it not strange concerning the fiery trial which is to try you, as though some strange thing happened unto you: But rejoice, inasmuch as ye are partakers of Christ's sufferings; that, when his glory shall be revealed, ye may be glad also with exceeding joy."

God places a thumbprint in your heart, and He will show you who you are supposed to be. He places desires within each one of us. Those desires are intertwined with the very fibers of who you are.

It's Godronic to think that our desire is somehow our *own* desire. It's not, God placed that desire *in* you. That's what He is talking about in His word when he says in Psalms 37:4 says, "Delight yourself in the Lord and He will give you the desires of your heart." Meaning, He is placing them in you. We think He is going to allow us that cheeseburger we want to eat and not gain those calories from it. Again, He is not a genie in a bottle. He gives us the desires so that we will walk them out, which in turn means we are walking in His will.

My prayer for you is that this chapter will help you find what your true identity is. If you know our Heavenly Father as your personal Savior, the biggest hurdle is already overcome. The next thing is to see what the Lord says about you.

I am an identical twin and for the longest time I thought that we had the same exact DNA. As you can see, I was not a biology major in school. My twin sister, Lisa, and I wanted to know what our actual DNA was, so we sent our DNA to Ancestry.com. I was a little shocked to see the differences. I had a little more Irish in me, which explains my fiery temper, while she has a little more Great Britain ancestry, which explains her sense of fashion...ha ha. My point is, even though we are identical twins, we still have our very own DNA, or differences that make us special.

So, if God created us to be so different, why do we compare ourselves to one another? Keep in mind that **comparison is the thief of identity!** So, why do we try our hardest, almost selling our souls to the Devil, to try and mimic someone else? Or to have something someone else has? I'm sure we are all guilty of that. I know I have done that my entire life comparing myself to my twin and my older sister.

I always felt that Lisa got the better hair gene. Her thick voluptuous hair is something I have envied my entire life. As for my older sister Ruth, I have been green with envy my entire life of her legs. I can hit the gym five days a week and still never have her gorgeous legs. I know—covet! Covet! Covet! Lord forgive me.

But God made me the way He wanted me. When those voices start chattering at me, I just remember what God has said: "I don't make mistakes. What you see as imperfect I made for a reason. Trust me that I made the *best* you possible. I made you in *MY* image, not in the image of anyone else."

So why do we do that? Why do we compare ourselves to others? Or what they look like? Or what we lack? I'll tell you why. It's because we aren't listening to the one that created us or what the Bible says in Psalm 139:14, "I praise you because I am fearfully and *wonderfully made...*"

Keep in mind that this does not give us a free pass to neglect what God gave us. If we don't take care of His temple, then who will?

When we trust the voice of God, we start seeing things in the spiritual realm. And friends, let me tell you, this is an amazing place to be. This is the place of complete freedom.

Let's take a look at little Annie, a five-year-old little girl. Her parents were divorcing because of her father's alcohol use and his need for other women in his life. What Annie doesn't see is that when her dad doesn't live with her anymore that it has nothing to do with her and she soon blames herself.

Annie's dad starts neglecting his daily phone calls to her. His visits become fewer and farther between. His words begin to mean very little when his promises to see her end with excuses of having to work. Annie is now carrying the baggage of being an orphan at the age of five even though her father is not physically dead.

She doesn't deserve this treatment from her dad, yet she is stuck carrying around the orphan spirit and it seems to shape who she is growing up.

As she grows up, this orphan spirit attaches itself very deep to her and holds on for dear life. It makes her view herself as never being good enough. It lies to her that men don't stick around. She soon finds herself doing anything to win the approval of men. She displays behavior of clinginess and distrust of men.

It's not until she grows up and finds the Lord that she realizes that she has carried this orphan spirit around for years. It is then that she decides she wants her full identity back and she doesn't want the label as "Little Orphan Annie" anymore.

There are thousands of stories just like Annie's. A child loses a parent by death and absorbs the orphan spirit. Another person doesn't know their parents at all and lives with an orphan spirit. What about that person who tries desperately to win the approval of a parent, but the parent just doesn't care? Or a wife that is neglected by her husband while she constantly tries to gain his attention? Or the little boy that witnesses the favoritism his sister receives from their parents? Or the mom that has to work three jobs to make ends meet and is missing out on life? What about the person who feels orphaned by God because he or she doesn't know Him personally, or at all, for that matter?

You see the orphan spirit comes with many different faces. But the end result is the same: a lack of identity.

The only way to heal from an orphaned spirit is to acknowledge that it is present. The following are signs of an orphaned spirit:

- *A person walks around with a spirit of rejection and abandonment.*

- *A person unconsciously assumes that people are against him or her.*

- *Those with an orphan spirit have rarely or never been affirmed by a father or mother; therefore, they are always striving to prove themselves to others.*

- *They constantly strive to succeed and to feel significant.*

- *They elevate themselves above others so they can feel good about themselves.*

- *They don't know how to emotionally connect with other people.*

- *They do not feel good about themselves.*

- *They do not know how to treat others; people with an orphan spirit often mistreat and or abuse others.*

- *They do not interpret reality correctly. I have found that those who carry an orphan spirit interpret everything through the lenses of their abandonment, rejection, and disappointment.*

- *They are always looking for approval and recognition.*

- *Those with an orphan spirit have a huge hole in their heart that only God can fill.*

- *Work and accomplishments are often at the center of their life.*

- *They have a difficult time relating to God as their Father because they either view God as a harsh taskmaster or as a distant father who cannot be fully trusted.*

My question is this: Can you relate to any of these signs? Or for that matter, did you relate to all of them? When you read those words, did they resonate with your spirit? Have you carried around an orphaned spirit that you want to see yourself free from? Do you know someone close to you who exhibits these signs?

I'm going to be honest. This chapter was extremely difficult for me because I didn't feel I truly understood what was involved with an orphaned spirit until I dug a little deeper. And when I dug deeper, I realized that each and every person can probably relate to having an orphaned spirit in some way or another. Some of us may be able to pinpoint what brought it on and some of us may not have a clue.

Whether you can relate to one thing on the list of indicators of an orphaned spirit, or you are ready to call LifeLock because you feel someone stole your complete identity, God is ready to restore you.

Now that we have identified it and what the definition is, how do we get rid of it? Simple: We see what God has to say about you. First, remember what I said earlier: *When you realize what you possess, it is then that you find your true identity.*

Second, I'm going to say this prayer and I invite you to say it with me:

"Dear Heavenly Father, I am asking that you forgive my sins so that I can come before you with a clean heart. I am asking that you help me identify in my life where the orphaned spirit gained access. I trust that once we have identified the access point, you will come along with me on this journey to shut the door. If I need to forgive someone, please help me release the bitterness and resentment I may be holding on to so that I can forgive. Show me how to fully let it go so I can be made whole. I am fully aware of your love for me and that you only want the best for me, so as we

walk this journey together, help me see myself clearly
through your eyes only. As you restore me, I trust that
each wound that brought me to this point will have
your healing touch and that I will finally be able to
walk in the fullness of you. Amen."

If you prayed that prayer, get ready for God to start revealing things to you that you may have been unaware of before. This is a good thing. Follow the process that God designs for you. Trust that He knows you more intimately than anyone else in the entire world and He only wants good for you.

He will reveal to you what your personal specifics are for this process:

- *What you need to pinpoint and identify;*

- *What you need to address and act on;*

- *What is involved in your healing process;*

- *How God wants you to recover; and*

- *How to flourish in this next chapter of your life.*

Once these have been addressed and prayed over, trust that the Lord will bring you to a place of healing that He designed specifically for you. Spend some quality time with Him so he can begin to show you who you are through His eyes. This was one of my most revealing times with Him because He showed me what His heart really looked like toward me, and boy 'ol boy, this was absolutely life changing. I'm sure this will be life changing for you too.

RED ROVER, RED ROVER, SEND SATAN RIGHT OVER!

Once we agree to allow God to completely take over and take our baggage, the Devil can't win. He can't torment us anymore. Why? Because when we see God holding our hand walking this journey with us, it is then that we have the full confidence that we will have what we ask of Him. That's why the Bible says in Hebrews 4:16, "Let us therefore come *boldly* unto the throne of grace that we may obtain mercy and find grace to help in time of need."

Once we realize what we contain and what we have access to, that is where our boldness comes out like a lion. No more will we play patty cake with the Devil. From here on out it's, "Red rover, red rover, send Satan right over!"

For too long we have allowed the enemy to beat us up and keep us prisoners in this sick game where he appears to have the upper hand. But Friends, he's a liar and the father of lies! We have the creator of the universe just waiting to be invited into this game. And guess what—spoiler alert—we are on the winning team!

I absolutely giggle out loud thinking about what I have access to. Maybe because the enemy kept me blind for so long. I felt so defeated that most days—OK, let's be honest—for years I wouldn't even try. I just tried not to make too many waves so that Satan didn't notice me. When he didn't notice me I thought I really wasn't a threat to him. I was deceived into believing that he was leaving me alone. *Wrong!*

One of his key strategies is keeping us quiet, complacent, and doing nothing! But that is not God's design for our lives.

When we listen to what God says about us, the picture of our identity becomes crystal clear. This is what He says about us:

- *We can never be separated from God's love (Romans 8:39).*

- *We have wisdom from God (1 Corinthians 1:30).*

- *Our labor is not in vain (1 Corinthians 15:58).*

- *He calls us His treasured possession (Deuteronomy 7:6).*

- *We are a new creation (2 Corinthians 5:17).*

- *We become God's children (Galatians 3:26).*

- *He calls us His heir (Romans 8:17).*

- *We have every spiritual blessing (Ephesians 1:3).*

- *We have the forgiveness of sins (Ephesians 1:7).*

- *We were also chosen (Ephesians 1:11).*

- *We are for His praise and His glory (Ephesians 1:12).*

- *We have been seated in the heavenly realms (Ephesians 2:6).*

- *We've been given the incomparable riches of God's grace (Ephesians 2:7).*

- *We who were once far away have been brought near (Ephesians 2:13).*

- *We are built together as a holy building (Ephesians 2:22).*

- *We may approach God with freedom and confidence (Ephesians 3:12).*

- *He calls us His workmanship (Ephesians 2:10).*

- *We are light (Ephesians 5:8).*

- *Our joy overflows (Philippians 1:26).*

- *All our needs are met according to His glorious riches (Philippians 4:19).*

- *We have our hope of glory (Colossians 1:27).*

- *We are rooted and built up (Colossians 2:7).*

- *We have been given the fullness of the deity (Colossians 2:9- 10).*

- *We can give thanks in all circumstances (1 Thessalonians 5:18).*

- *We have faith, hope, and love (1 Timothy 1:1, 14).*

- *We have the promise of life (2 Timothy 1:1).*

- *He calls us His sons and daughters (Corinthians 6:18).*

So, as you can see, God thinks very highly of us, and He should because we were made in His image. If we are not mindful of who God says we are, it is easy for the enemy to slip in and deceive us about who we are and what we possess, and the Devil will lie and tell us that we possess *nothing!* He is a liar!

You see, if you have asked God into your heart then you know that we are on the winning team. The Lord has already won the battle; we just need to accept what He is giving us. If you haven't asked God into your life and would like to do that right now, flip to the last page of this book where I have a prayer waiting just for you!

When you know the spirit of God is living on the inside, nothing compares to that. Get ready, My Dear, you are in for the time of your life! This is where healing begins.

Rough and Crusty...

Have you ever wondered why the Bible lists a person's lineage when he or she is mentioned? I have. And I feel it's because knowing who you came from is extremely important.

For example, take the man named Jahaziel. You more than likely haven't heard of him, and if you have, you have dug deep into God's word. Jahaziel is tucked away in 2 Chronicles, Chapter 20.

The Bible says in verse 14, "The Spirit of the Lord came upon Jahaziel, son of Zechariah, the son of Bennaiah, the son of Jeiel, the son of Mattaniah, a Levite and descendant of Asaph, as he stood in the assembly."

If you are like me, I have more times than I care to admit, breezed right by all of the "sons of..." until the Lord directed me to investigate why he listed this lineage and what is in a name.

Well, let's take a quick look at the meaning of the names:

Jahaziel means: God sees
Zechariah means: The Lord has remembered
Bennaiah means: Yahweh build up
Jeiel means: Snatched away by God
Mattaniah means: Gift or hope of the Lord
Asaph means: Who gathers together

If we replace the name with only its meaning, it reads like this: "The Spirit of the Lord came upon 'God sees,' 'The Lord has remembered,' 'Yahweh builds up,' 'Snatched away by God,' 'Gift or hope of the Lord,' 'Who gathers together,' as he stood in the assembly."

See how differently something looks by seeing what God has to say about a person? When we see God saying, He sees, He remembers, He builds up, He is snatching us away, He is our hope and He gathers us

127

together, it is then that we start seeing His heart toward us. This is the beginning of shaping your new identity into the one that matches how God really sees you.

When you can allow your mind to rest on who God says you are instead of who you say you are, or who the world says you are, then your rebuilding process is fully underway.

If you are curious like me, you have probably already put this book down, went over to your phone or computer, and typed your name in to see what the meaning is. Because let's face it, we all want to feel special. We want to see if we are a Jahaziel, or a Joshua, which means Jehovah is generous, or a William, which means determined protector, or a Timothy, which means honoring God, or a Joel, which means Yahweh is God, or a Benjamin which means son of my right hand, or a Jeffrey, which means peaceful protector.

My name, Lori, means laurel tree or sweet bay tree (symbols of honor and victory). I was truly humbled when I saw that and that made me dig a little deeper.

A laurel wreath (which is made from the leaves from the laurel tree) is a symbol of victory and honor. It is a round (which never ends) wreath made of interlocking branches and leaves. In ancient Greece wreaths were awarded to victors. This was fascinating to me.

But what happens when you see that your name means something like a scab? Scab? Really? Yep, there is a man in the Bible whose name is Gareb, and the meaning of his name is scab. Can you imagine this poor man walking around knowing his name means a dry, rough protective crust that forms over a cut or wound during healing?

Well, you could either view it pessimistically or optimistically, your choice. I know you're saying to yourself, "How in the world is there something positive about that name?" Well, I'll show you.

When something is hurt, cut, scraped, broken open, scratched, or severed, there *has* to be a scab to heal that wound. There is nothing else that can take the place of a scab. You see, there is no replacing Gareb. There is no substitute for Gareb. There is nothing else like Gareb. Gareb is so uniquely special that he was chosen to be the covering over a hurt. Kind of Christlike, don't you think?

Gareb is the protective outer layer. He's dry, rough, and he has a disgusting name. He is all the things that no one in his right mind would want to be identified with, let alone be defined by. *But,* Gareb is being used to do something that no one else can do! Astonishing to see how God works, isn't it? I'll bet you are wishing you were a little rough and crusty now, don't you!

I know you see where I am going with this. It's the epitome of the underdog story. And who doesn't like an underdog story? What the world sees as disgusting and nasty, God sees as the potential of being Christlike. Astonishing isn't it?

Take the story of Zadok. I found this guy while digging into the story of David. While reading about the warriors that joined David, I noticed something a little special about him.

Bear with me, this gets extremely interesting. 1 Chronicles 12:22-37 says, "The Bible says that day after day men came to help David, until he had a great army, like the army of God. These are the number of the men armed for battle who came to David at Hebron to turn Saul's kingdom over to him, as the Lord had said:

- *Men of Judah, carrying shield and spear - 6,800 armed for battle*

- *Men of Simeon, warriors ready for battle - 7,100*

- *Men of Levi - 4,600, including Jehoiada, leader of the family of Aaron, with - 3,700 men, and Zadok, A brave young warrior, with 22 officers from his family*

- *Men of Benjamin, Saul's kinsmen - 3,000*

- *Men of Ephraim, brave warriors, famous in their own clans - 20,800*

- *Men of half the tribe of Manasseh, designated by name to come and make David king - 18,000*

- *Men of Issachar, who understood the times and knew what Israel should do - 200*

- *Men of Zebulun, experienced solders prepared for battle with every type of weapon to help David - 50,000*

- *Men of Naphtali, 1,000 officers together with men carrying sword and shield - 37,000*

- *Men of Dan, ready for battle - 28,600*

- *Men of Asher, experienced soldiers prepared for battle - 40,000*

- *Men of Rueben, Gad, and half the tribe of Manasseh, armed with every type of weapon, - 120,000*

Did you notice Zadok? Zadok only brought 22 officers with him. Twenty-two! He brought 22 of the 340,822 men listed. That is only 0.006455 percent of the total. Yet he was found worthy enough to be listed among those bringing weapons, warriors who were famous among their own clans, experienced solders, chiefs, etc.

He was characterized as being brave and young. Who wants to be categorized as being young when you are trying to be big and bad, rough and tough, ready to fight in a battle? Not me.

Everyone else brought hundreds or thousands of men. Yet Zadok brought twenty-two men and was found worthy enough to be listed among the others.

I'm sure your mind is racing like mine was when I stumbled upon this little gem. How does someone who is not part of the family, with a small, puny entourage end up getting his name printed in black and white in the Bible? I'll tell you how, because God doesn't look at the most liked, the most popular, or the richest. He looks at the little that someone is offering and puts it up there with the elite, so that it's considered elite as well. God is no respecter of persons. He's not keeping score of who brought what or how many. He looked at the heart of the man, and *that* is why Zadok made the cut. I have to tell you that these underdog stories really fire me up!

Do you understand what is happening here? God wants to show you that your "little" is much when you give it to Him. He wants to show you that no matter how orphaned you feel, you will always have a seat at His table. He wants to show you that when you think you don't have enough; you have plenty as long as you put Him in charge of it.

He put Zadok's twenty-two officers into an army of more than 340,000. God didn't expect Zadok to fight alone. That's why He sent His covering. In this instance, His covering was more than 340,000 men!

So when you feel like you don't measure up or that God can't use you, or that you are a nobody, be careful my dear, He may just be setting you up for the greatest adventure of your life!

A Dirty Dollar...

In these few stories I have shared with you I am showing you the epitome of God's heart toward you, whether you have had an orphaned spirit that you have carried around for years, you feel small and undeserving, or you feel you are unseen and unimportant. God doesn't take the face value of something and turn away, repulsed. He does just the opposite.

If allowed, He will take the widowed, the hurting, the orphaned, the shunned, the puny, the neglected, and the scarred and turn them into His masterpiece.

My pastor, Tim Oldfield, gave this analogy once and it has stuck with me for years. He took a hundred dollar bill out of his pocket, crumbled it up and threw it on the ground. Then he pulled a gentleman out of the congregation and asked him to come forward. The man was asked to go over and step on that hundred dollar bill. The gentleman looked puzzled at Pastor Oldfield but did what he requested. Pastor Oldfield then asked the gentleman to go over to it and stomp on it, pick it up and throw it up in the air and let it fall to the ground. The gentleman looked at my pastor like he was crazy, but he picked up the hundred dollar bill, threw it up in the air, let it fall, and then stomped on it.

Pastor Oldfield then walked over to the hundred dollar bill, held it in his hand all rolled up in a ball and asked this question: "Is the hundred dollar bill ruined?" The congregation said "no." Pastor Oldfield then asked, "Does the hundred dollar bill still have its value?" The congregation said "Yes, of course it does."

You see, Pastor Oldfield was showing us that something of great value doesn't lose it's worth or value because it's dirty, misused, stomped on, and scarred up a little bit. That money had the same value it did before someone tried to deface it.

God is showing us that no matter what we have faced or been through, our value doesn't change. My prayer is that you fully comprehend that our mistakes and our past does not define us. What matters is that we decide to allow the Lord to put us on that pedestal we so deserve to be on.

When you realize who your daddy is, your eyes will shift to your new identity and see that God has called you by name and the name He is saying is, "Mine!"

So as you have acknowledged, analyzed, brought out of hiding, sought forgiveness for and are recognizing your new identity, my prayer for you is this:

"Dear Heavenly Father, I come to you with a thankful heart because you have been faithful through this entire process with each one of your sons and daughters. As they begin their life of freedom, I ask that you fill that empty void where you washed everything away and give them beauty for ashes. Anoint them as your sons and daughters and speak words of truth to them—truth about them being set free and allowing them to walk in that freedom. Show them how to never accept defeat again from the Devil and that they have full authority in every situation to claim the ground you have set before them. Allow them to have full confidence that when the enemy comes at them in one direction, by your name he must flee from them in seven. Show each one of your sons and daughters that you are going to heal even the most desolate places in their hearts. Thank you for allowing your sons and daughters to enjoy this restoration process with you! You are truly our conquering king. Amen."

~ Another link has been broken ~

CHAPTER 8
RESTING AT HIS FEET

———————

I n this final chapter we will look at the benefits of "resting at the Lord's feet." We will address why this is truly a peaceful place to be and how God designed us to trust in Him by just resting. Once we fully comprehend this mindset, our faith skyrockets!

The definition of rest is this: cease work or movement in order to relax, refresh oneself, or recover strength; be placed or supported so as to stay in a specified position.

When I read the definition of resting, I can't help but see myself as a little girl wrapped up in the bottom part of Jesus' robe sleeping, and I don't have a care in the world. What an awesome place to be.

But, if you are anything like me, and Lord I hope to goodness you are not that hardheaded, you have had a difficult time understanding the concept of "resting at His feet." It is even quite possible that you have never even heard this phrase before.

This lesson was the most difficult to grasp in my entire walk with the Lord because it required trust. With my past, trust was something that didn't come easily.

There comes a time in everyone's life when this great epiphany takes place; when we realize that there is nothing left to do except trust God and rest at His feet. If you have already learned this, then congratulations, you have obviously overcome a huge mountain in your life.

My sister, Lisa, and my dad used to tell me to "rest at his feet" so many times, I thought I would scream. They would tell me over and over and over again, "Lori, when you have done all you know to do, you just have to trust God and rest at His feet."

As much as it frustrated me to hear those words chime in my ears over and over again, I'm sure it was even more frustrating to them trying to teach little ol' me how to get the Lord's peace by just resting. So, I'm sending out a huge shout out and dedicating this chapter to all the Lisas and dads out there and for all of their endless cheerleading!

I am just going to put this out there: I am a hyper person. Had I been born a decade or two later I'm certain I would have been diagnosed with severe ADHD. No joke, it's extremely difficult for me to even keep my thoughts together enough to make a clear sentence.

So when Lisa or my dad would tell me to rest at His feet, I took it literally as if I had to lie around and have the Lord hand-feed me grapes while I sat on my couch just resting. I know this may seem foreign to you, but in my mind, I could not grasp the concept at all. I would explain to them, "Guys, I am resting, but I just feel like I need to help God along because he is not doing things in my timeframe!"

I couldn't fully comprehend what the phrase meant. Then, one day after *years* of complaining about my life and the situation I was in at the time, my sister Lisa looked over at me, grinned, and quietly said, "When you totally get the concept, it's going to change your life." I wanted to smack her. I got aggravated because I still didn't get it. I said I got it. I thought I got it. I even got desperate enough one night while lying in my bed that I closed my eyes and pictured myself lying at the feet of Jesus. This worked while I had my eyes closed, but the second my eyes popped open, boom, I picked up my troubles again and continued being annoyed at life...again!

I'm certain you can relate to the mentality of picking up your baggage that you *just* handed over to the Lord. I'm sure you have even gone outside of your family and friends for advice and lashed out on social media. Don't be offended. I have done the very same thing. I can bet that I even posted a sarcastic meme that described exactly how I felt. Something like, "I'm not saying I hate you, but I would unplug your life support to charge my phone," or "Some people just need a high-five! In the face! With a chair!" But to be honest, this only heightens the situation, especially when the post only receives eight likes.

Somehow it makes us feel better when we try to purge our emotional garbage and hope that someone will respond with an encouraging message. But to be honest, the encouraging few words we receive is not going to change our situation. It may make us feel better momentarily, but the only situation changer is the Lord.

I'm going to sum it up for you so that you don't have to read the entire chapter wondering what this phrase means. Resting at his feet means that you *know* nothing will come to you that the Lord has not allow. And if He allows it, then you must know He already has a plan for you. It is resting in the fact that God only wants the best for you. It is *knowing* that He loves you. He is fighting for you even when you don't see it. It is trusting Him to do what is right and just even when we don't deserve it.

Resting at His feet means that no matter what, He has your back. It means that what the enemy has set up for your demise, the Lord will use it to benefit you. It is knowing beyond a shadow of a doubt that He is someone who will rip the Heavens open to come to your rescue. When you start seeing God as someone you have an intimate personal relationship with, the idea of resting at His feet comes more into focus. And what you focus on, grows. What you feed, grows. When you focus on your relationship with the Lord instead of the dire situation you are facing, peace kicks in. When you nurture those emotions, it gets easier and easier to rest at His feet. When we focus on how good God is, it becomes much easier to see how He works in our lives.

HUNGRY LIKE A WOLF...

There is a story I heard years ago that stuck with me, so I'll share it with you.

An old Cherokee man is teaching his grandson about life. "A fight is going on inside me," he said to the boy. "It is a terrible fight and it is between two wolves. One is evil–he is anger, envy, sorrow, regret, greed, arrogance, self-pity, guilt, resentment, inferiority, lies, false pride, superiority, and ego."

He continued, "The other is good–he is joy, peace, love, hope, serenity, humility, kindness, benevolence, empathy, generosity, truth, compassion, and faith.

The same fight is going on inside you, and inside every other person, too."

The grandson thought about it for a minute and then asked his grandfather, "Which wolf will win?"

The old Cherokee man simply replied, "The one you feed."

When you feed yourself the Word of God and listen to what He has to say about you, those are the very things that will start to grow inside of you. Joy will start to grow. Love will start to grow. Kindness will start to grow. Hope will start to grow. Before you know it, you will be the very conduit the Lord needs to turn this world upside down!

It is absolutely the best feeling in the world when we learn to see how God moves in every situation, and how it will only benefit us.

There was a defining moment for me when the Lord gave me spiritual insight that allowed me to rest in the fact that I knew He had everything under control. The story is about my son, Justin.

As a Christian mom I believe it is a natural process to pray for our children. We pray that they will grow up to love and serve the Lord. My daughter, Jordan, always seemed to have a natural love for God and it came very easy for her to have that relationship with Him. My son,

Justin, on the other hand, required a little more dedication in prayer on my behalf so that he, too, would have that relationship.

The older Justin got, the more he seemed to want to make his own decisions on the whole religion thing. This broke my heart because his choice was not to serve God whole heartedly. The Devil was lying to him telling him that if he knew *about God*, he was doing all he needed to do...the other "religious stuff" was just hypocritical church stuff.

When he turned fifteen my prayers intensified, I truly believe this was the prompting of the Lord. The harder I prayed for him, the more Justin seemed repulsed by religion. Of course, this only brought up fears from my childhood and how I turned away from God and walked my own unsaved journey. I was determined not to allow this to happen to Justin.

Of course, I allowed the enemy to beat me up with fear as I bought into his lies that Justin would not ever want a relationship with the Lord. It seemed that other things in his life were more appealing to him. After feeling defeated for a short time, I felt the Lord whisper in my spirit, "I have the final say, keep the faith, continue to pray for him and watch what I do." This was the Lord showing me to keep my ear tuned to him and not the Devil. This armed me for battle, and I was ready to fight!

This went on for months. The harder I prayed and fasted for Justin, the more he seemed angered and repulsed by religion. He and I began drifting apart and didn't have the relationship we once had, and this broke my heart. I'm sure, had I seen what was taking place in the spirit realm, I would have seen our spirits warring against each other. It was a battle of good and evil.

One night, as our family was preparing to host a revival, things got even worse. Justin had informed me that he was not going to attend the revival. Let me just tell you, I don't take kindly to my kids "telling" me what they are and are not going to do. But I knew I had to handle this situation with kid gloves.

So, he and I sat down one evening and discussed why he didn't want to go. He gave all the usual excuses, "It's not my thing...I already made plans...I don't want to be forced to do something I don't want to do..." You name it, he said it. After hearing him out on the matter, I said I respected his opinion, but it was my decision, and he was going to go. Oh, let me tell ya, that boy has my DNA for sure. His fiery temper came out. He ended the conversation with, "You can't force me to go...I want to move in with my dad" and out the door he went. Of course, this left me bawling and freaking out, wondering what in the world had I just done. I began second guessing myself and the entire situation.

Later that evening around 11:30 p.m., my family was still at prayer night preparing for the revival and my daughter came over to me and said that Justin was at home and wanted to talk to me. Of course, I thought Justin was going to fall on his knees and accept the Lord right then and there...wrong.

I walk in the door and he and I began talking. He apologized for leaving the way he did and explained that he didn't want this situation to define our relationship. He began explaining to me, *again,* that religion was just not his thing. As we looked at each other with tears streaming down our cheeks, the Lord pulled the veil back and I was able to see things spiritually.

The warring Justin and I had been going through the last several months was the enemy fighting for Justin's soul and dividing us so that Justin was isolated. This was a very bizarre thing to experience. The more he cried and gave excuses, the more I began to see it was the enemy running in fear! The enemy did *not* want Justin at that revival! I sat there listening to him cry and give every excuse as to why he didn't want to go but I couldn't help but giggle at this point. I had the enemy freaking out...my prayers had been working! When the Lord revealed this to me, I began asking Justin more questions. I asked why he suddenly within the last several months had become so repulsed at the idea of having a relationship with the Lord and asked him what had changed so much. He used to go to church and not complain too much about it, but now it was a battle every week. Every Sunday morning, he would call from his dad's house and make up some excuse about why he couldn't make it to church. Why the sudden change? When Justin couldn't explain the change, it confirmed what the Lord had shown me. My constant praying was changing things! There was an all-out spiritual war going on for Justin's soul, and I was determined that God was going to win!

All the little personal words the Lord had given me over the last several months came rushing in and swirling around in my mind. The Bible verse I came across at the perfect time, Joshua 24:15, "But as for me and my household, we will serve the Lord." Man oh man, I quoted that scripture a million times walking through my house praying for Justin. The perfect song that would come on the radio when I felt the prompting of God to pray for him. The peace I felt as I prayed over his room anointing it with oil while he was in school. God was showing me His heart in this situation and that He had everything under control. This allowed me to start resting in the fact that I knew the Lord had everything under control.

At the end of our conversation that night, Justin promised he would attend the revival, which he did. He didn't accept the Lord at that time, but I knew the Lord had a hold of him and was tugging at his heart because he could only stand to be there for about forty-five minutes before he headed out the door. I can't explain the peace I felt about the situation, but I knew beyond what my mind could fathom and what my physical eyes could see that the Lord was working on him, which was why Justin was so miserable. This allowed me to rest in the Lord like I never had done before.

This was one of the most difficult times of my life because I thought I was going to lose the relationship I had with my son. I thought he was going to move out and be dead-set against a true relationship with the Lord. But you see what the Lord did, He showed me *His* heart and how to rest in the fact that He had everything under control. The Lord told me that He loves Justin even more than I do and He was answering my prayers, in His timing. I wasn't freaking out or fretting anymore. I don't know how to explain it, other than to say that a person's spirit is completely at rest when he relies on the Lord. I had done what I knew to do; I prayed, I counseled Justin the best way I knew how with the guidance from the Holy Spirit, and I left the rest up to God.

My prayers continued for Justin in a way that thanked God for constantly keeping him in the forefront of his mind. I knew that he had Justin in the palm of His hand and at just the right time, Justin would have all defenses taken down and would accept the Lord into his heart. I thanked God for the peace He gave me in this situation because I knew the Lord would not stop chasing him down until he was saved. The Lord gave me the scripture in Luke 15:4, "Suppose one of you has a hundred sheep and loses one of them. Doesn't he leave the ninety-nine in the open country and go after the one lost sheep until he finds it?" This is how we learn to rest in the Lord, applying His word to every situation and knowing that if He said it, you can be certain it *will* come to pass.

Nine weeks after the revival had ended, Justin walked up to the altar at church one Sunday in December and accepted the Lord as his personal Savior. The joy that I felt in that moment was something I still cannot find words to describe. I now had joy and peace in this situation and let me just say that there is nothing like that combination of contentment. The Lord has begun fulfilling every prayer I have ever spoken over Justin.

I have shared this story with you so you can see that it is usually the time that you are facing your biggest storms that you will learn to rest in the Lord. I am not going to lie and say this was an easy trial to go through, because it wasn't. But once that trust factor kicks in with the Lord, he will show you how He is working in your situation, which in turn allows you to rest in the situation.

If you are in the process of learning how to lean on the Lord in situations and to rest at His feet, I invite you to say this prayer with me:

> *"Dear Heavenly Father, I thank you that I can come boldly to the throne room of heaven and present my heavy heart to you. Lord, I ask that you remove all doubt, fear, and unbelief and allow me to see you as a loving father who only wants the best for me. As your word says in Proverbs 3:5-6, 'Trust in the LORD with all your heart and lean not on your own understanding; in all your ways submit to him, and he will make your paths straight.' Lord, allow me to see you in every situation working things out beautifully on my behalf. I am speaking these words in faith; I trust you, and I will continue doing what I know to do based on your word. I will allow you full control in my life and I welcome your peace to rest on me so that I can in turn rest at your feet. In all these things, I give you thanks and honor. In Jesus's name I pray, Amen."*

TABLE FOR TWO, PLEASE...

As we begin trusting God in our situations so that we can rest in him, it makes it easier if we look at what He has done for others in the past. So let's take a look at the Biblical story of Hananiah (Shadrach), Mishael (Meshach), and Azariah (Abednego). Now, them boys knew what being in a heated situation really meant. They refused to bow down to King Nebuchadnezzar and worship him. Therefore, they were thrown into the fiery furnace that was turned up seven times hotter than normal. Yet the Lord delivered them out of that furnace unharmed–without so much as a single hair on their heads being singed.

What about the story of Daniel in the lion's den? The story teaches us about the faithfulness of God, even if we feel like God has forgotten us. Daniel was thrown into the lion's den with starving lions and was there overnight. Now, how are you going to rest at the Lord's feet when you have lions nipping at yours? But Daniel did in fact rest at the Lord's feet. He trusted that the Lord would deliver him out of the den unharmed, and He did.

What about the story of Lazarus? The man was dead for crying out loud. How much more final can a situation be? Yet Jesus raised him from the dead. Why did Jesus wait until Lazarus had died before appearing on the scene? I believe it was for people to see a miracle instead of a healing.

Being in a difficult situation doesn't mean you are fearless. I'm sure if we had the opportunity to ask the three Hebrew men if they were fearful, they would probably tell us they were. I'm certain Daniel was fearful as well. Maybe they felt fearful and as though they were going to die when they looked at their situation and didn't see a way out. But they kept their faith and rested at the feet of the Lord. And guess what? God got them out of their situation...unharmed!

You see, when you think your situation has overtaken you and God has forgotten where you are, that's the enemy lying again. *You* have the power through Christ to shut the mouth of the enemy and trust in the fact that God said He would never leave you nor forsake you.

And when God says something, well folks, that's about as certain as anything can be!

When you get to the point that you know the Lord will move that mountain for you, fix the situation you are in, make the impossible possible, change that doctor's report, stretch that last dollar in your wallet, remove that addiction you have suffered with for years, put that broken marriage back together again better than it was before, resurrect that dead thing in your life, that is true peace and resting at His feet. We are not dealing with a finite God with limited resources. No, we have the creator of the universe on our side and He is so madly in love with us that He sacrificed His one and only Son so that we could spend an eternity with Him. That is true love. That's who you have fighting for you. So, pull up a seat because the Lord is serving dinner at a table for two, and guess what, He invited your enemies to watch!

It's Raining Fish. Yes, Fish!

Are you still doubting that God will work in your situation? Or that it's too hard for Him to fix whatever it is you are dealing with and that you just can't seem to rest at His feet? If so, let's take a look at the people who live in the Australian town of Lajamanu.

I'm going to let you in on a little secret. I absolutely love to fish! I love everything about it. I love the smell of the air during fishing season. I love the way the water sparkles in the sunshine like diamonds. I love watching an occasional fish jump out of the water just to show me that the underwater world is alive and ready to play. I love the way my fishing line sounds when I have hooked a big fish and it starts taking my line out. I love the tugging sensation when there is a sizeable fish on the other end of my pole. I love it all!

So, when I heard the story of a place where it was raining fish, I have to be honest, it sounded like a dream come true. I was ready to grab my fishing pole and head out the door to witness this miracle firsthand!

This little phenomenon took place in a tiny Australian desert town about 300 miles away from the nearest river. The 670 residents witnessed fish falling from the sky for two days. Is this true? Yes, it is. I have to be honest, I would have loved to have interviewed the people that lived there to see who prayed for food. Then I would like to shake the hand of the individuals who had enough faith to pray for– of all things–fish! We don't know if in fact someone prayed for fish, but that's what they got. It's not like they prayed for whatever food you find in the desert. No, praying for fish in the desert, well that's impossible! And impossible prayers are the ones that receive miracles! The news indicated that a storm sucked all the fish up in the sky to about 40,000-50,000 feet where they were frozen. Yet the report stated that some of the fish were alive when they were raining down.

Based on this information, some people analyzed it and dismissed it as a weather phenomenon. I'll give them that. It was indeed the weather that caused the fish to be sucked up into the sky. But who is the maker of the weather? Who hung the moon and the stars? Who told the ocean how far it could go and when its waves had to stop? I'll tell you who: God.

It doesn't make it any less of a miracle because people have figured out how to rationalize it in their minds and stick a weather label on it. It did in fact rain fish in the desert. Period.

I can just picture God almost belly laughing looking at the faces of those people as they saw fish fall from the sky. You see, He delights in us and He constantly looks for ways to bless us. He is searching for those who put all their trust in Him. Those are the ones that truly delight the Lord.

You see, the key to everything in life is this: your personal relationship with God. It's not religion. It's not being perfect so He will love you. It's not attending church on Sunday so you can mark it off of your to-do list. It's simply a relationship with Abba Father.

Resting in the fact that God himself has your situation already worked out should allow the peace of God to rest on you. That's what He wants from us, complete faith that He loves us and that His word is true. The Bible says in Romans 8:28, "And we know that in all things God works for the good of those who love him, who have been called according to his purpose."

Even when the Devil seems to have the upper hand in a situation, we should rest in the fact that God is not a liar and His word will not return void. God *will* work in that situation when we place Him in charge of it.

Let's keep in mind that we need to have God at the center of our lives and allow Him in the driver's seat. It's not fair to blame God for His absence in a situation when we have not given Him full access to it.

We carefully choose our accountants to handle our money. We trust the banker to count our money correctly. We trust the teachers in charge of teaching our children. We don't think twice about the school bus driver that takes our kids to school every day. We rely on Google as if it is the genius god.

So why not trust the Creator of the Universe to handle our situation? Let's face it, we should feel honored that God wants to be a part of our entire world and what is important to us. If He created everything, and knows everything, and is the epitome of love, why should we be fearful of handing over our situation to Him and doubt that He will work it out for His glory? The answer is simple: we shouldn't.

Once we learn to rest in God and realize that He is pleased when we have enough faith to hand it all over to Him and just breathe, that is when you will find your breakthrough.

SWEET BABY RUTH...

Why do you think God created us to sleep every day? Do you ever wonder why he didn't create us to just go, go, go all the time? I have asked myself this very thing many times. Because let's face it, we are a busy society that is almost addicted to busyness. I often said I wish God created us to never sleep so we could get more done. Thank you, Lord, for those unanswered prayers!

God is perfect in all His ways and He designed us that way for a reason. We tend to think of sleep as a time when the mind and body shut down. But in researching the purpose of sleep, I read that it is an active period in which a lot of important processing, restoration, and strengthening occurs.

Think about that for a minute. If we are constantly moving, doing, figuring, calculating, assessing, we can't rest. If our resting, and I'm speaking spiritually, causes solidification, restoration, and strengthening, why don't we rest more? I say sign me up for a daily nap on the couch!

Let's look at a newborn baby. We will call her Ruth. Ruth sleeps around sixteen to eighteen hours a day and doesn't have a care in the world. She cries and someone is rushing over to feed her. She trusts entirely that all her needs will be met and all she has to do is rest.

Look at how much she grows while resting! By the time she is about six months old, she has doubled her birth weight. Ah, sweet baby Ruth, this will be the only time in her life that she will not care about doubling her weight...ha ha.

My point in all of this is to show you how much a human can grow just by resting. Pretty fascinating, isn't it?

When we take our hands off the wheel and trust God, we allow Him to maneuver our situation and that's when we will grow the most. Our faith increases by allowing God to work in our lives. Resting at

His feet is the best place in the world to be.

When we have the greatest name in the entire world at our disposal, how can we possibly not rest? The name Jesus is like having a countless number of men in your army ready for battle. It's having the answers before being asked the question. It is knowing that no matter what you are faced with, the name Jesus is the answer.

There is just something about that name. It holds the power to wrestle the most evil demons, yet it's soft enough to comfort you when the world around you is crumbling.

When you call on the name of Jesus, all Hell is paralyzed. Think about that. The very demons that have tormented you are paralyzed when you utter the name of Jesus. When you realize what you have in your arsenal then you understand that you have the power of Heaven within you. With His name, Jesus, you have all you need to win this war you are in, and that will allow you to rest at His feet.

As we take charge of our life and stop allowing the enemy to beat us up, it is then that the Lord will show up and say, "Let me at 'em! I'm here to be the wrecking ball. I'm here to defeat what's before you and set the trap for the enemy! Just trust me!"

You see, it's releasing yourself from a prison that He didn't intend for you to live in. When you can praise Him no matter what you are facing because you know He has your back, it is then you can have peace in every situation. Having peace in every situation makes you joyful. When you are joyful then you have the strength of the Lord. And this is where God wants all of us to be: fully trusting Him in everything!

MOVING FORWARD...

As we have reached the last chapter and section in this book, it's not really an ending, but a beginning for you. It is designed as a "push-off" point for you. It's time to get out of the boat and get your feet wet.

It's time to move forward and do what God has called each of us to do. It's time to reach the lost and dying world that Satan has fought to keep enslaved. We need to allow God to grab us by the hand and move forward to start showing the world what He *really* looks like. When we are whole, and joyful and walking in what God has designed us to do, that's when we gain the attention of the lost. Remember, you may be the only "church" that someone sees.

It's setting yourself apart for God to work through, so people will crave what you carry. God created it to be that where there is light, there can't be darkness. We should seem so different to the people around us that they are drawn to us. In reality, they will be drawn to the Spirit of God we carry. That will be what changes the world.

If you are wondering what your calling is and how to start or continue in your journey with the Lord, it's identified in His Word. Remember to keep your ear tuned to Him. He will give you that desire. This is an exciting place to be...we should all dive in and see where the Lord leads each one of us.

We all want to have the one special gift that we so long for. Mine is singing. I have wanted a beautiful singing voice for as long as I can remember. I always tell people that if God were to grant my wish, I don't think I would ever just talk anymore, I would sing everything! But it appears that the Lord has decided I would be a more useful tool to him as a writer than a singer. But it doesn't stop me from belting out an old Loretta Lynn tune every once in a while as my kids just look at me and roll their eyes.

However, we are *all* called to preach the Gospel, as it says in Mark 16:15. We are *all* called to pray for our churches, pray for our leaders, and pray for our pastors (1 Timothy 2:1-3). We are *all* called to serve (I Peter 4:10-11). We are all called to pray for lost souls (Acts 26:18).

We are *all* called to move forward hand in hand with the lover of our soul.

In moving forward, we should keep in mind to do it in love. Love is not a feeling; it is a choice. My entire life I was under the impression that to be in love, I had to *feel* it...if I didn't feel it, then it wasn't love. This was a terrible misconception.

Love isn't something that you choose to do once and that's the end of it; it's a choice that we make every day. Some days it will come easy, and other days it won't. But love gives us spiritual eyes to see things the way the Lord sees them. And when we can see things through the eyes of God, wow, we are exactly where He wants us.

I'll share with you what was a complete game changer for me: it was picturing love like a beautifully wrapped present. It has exquisite shiny wrapping paper with a large beautiful red bow and a tag with my name on it. I can either choose to let it sit there unwrapped and to go to waste, or I can unwrap it and put it on and enjoy my gift from the Lord. The Bible says in I Thessalonians 5:8, "But since we belong to the day, let us be sober, *putting on faith and **love*** as a breastplate, and the hope of salvation as a helmet."

You see, it's something we put on, kind of like our very own Superman cape. Love is a force in the spirit realm that is as strong as death. It is a gift the Lord has freely given to us to use and to walk in. And I don't know about you, but I have always wanted to be a superhero. Once we put it on, we must activate it. We activate it by choosing to love in every situation, with every person by asking God to help us activate that part of His Spirit.

Choosing to love allows us to demonstrate grace with others. It reaches across the table of diversity that alienates and separates people. Love shows mercy when our carnal beings want to crucify them. Using love is the greatest force on the planet, and God shows us how to perfect it. When we allow love to be the first thing that comes out of our mouths and the first action we display, no Devil in Hell can combat it.

If this is your heart, I invite you to say this prayer:

"Lord, I come to you asking that you allow me to see my friends and family in their lost state so it keeps me on my face in prayer. Let me pray without ceasing and allow me to have the strength that can only come from you. Show me my limitations in the carnal realm and not try and obtain anything that is not from you. Unleash my tongue so that I can pray bold, fervent, heaven-shaking, demon-fleeing, life-changing, interceding prayers that will touch your heart and change the course of history for the very people you have placed in my life. God, I ask that you protect our pastors and leaders and give them courage to stand up for what is right in your eyes. Place people in their lives that love you, so they reflect the dignity that you desire to have displayed. Allow our churches to have a hunger for you again that can't be quenched. I ask that you open my spiritual eyes to see the gift of love that I can walk in every day. In all these things, I give you the glory and honor, Amen."

I am honored that you are ready to join me in pursuing lost souls. This is the greatest joy you will ever experience. As exhilarating as it was to experience your own awakening as you turned everything over to the Lord, the pure joy you feel when you are walking in what God has called you to do is indescribable.

When you allow God to do His perfect will in your life, His light will shine so brightly through you that people will be drawn to you.

People will want what you contain. That's the way the Lord designed it. If you have not already done so and would like to accept the Lord into your heart and to be saved, this is your time. This is why the Lord brought you to this very moment.

To be saved, you must confess that Jesus is Lord and acknowledge Him to have full reign over your life. You then need to invite Him into your heart to be the master controller.

I invite you to pray this prayer with me:

> *"Dear God, I realize that I am a sinner and I have sinned against you. I am asking for your forgiveness and invite you into my life. I acknowledge that you sent your Son to die on the cross for my sins and that He rose again and is alive today. I'm putting you in charge of my life so that your perfect will can be accomplished. From this moment forward I declare myself fully submitted to you. Prepare my heart to receive what you have in store for me because I am now ready to walk this journey with you. In Jesus' name I pray, Amen."*

If you prayed this prayer and truly meant it from your heart, congratulations, you are now a child of God and your life will never be the same again. I'm so proud of you and the faith you have already displayed by trusting God with your life.

What I suggest now is for you to share with someone what just happened to you. Let this person know that you just accepted Christ as your Lord and Savior. I would also strongly encourage you to get plugged in to a good Bible-based church and start reading the Bible every day. Whether it's one verse or an entire chapter, reading God's word is what will make you spiritually strong.

Now that you realize that the name of *Jesus is the key to everything in life,* then you, My Friend, have arrived and can rest at His feet. You are ready to embark upon the next chapter of life that God has set out before you.

~ Another link has been broken ~

LORI GLAZE

Lori has a passion for people in need which led her to the most remote locations in Uganda, Africa, the most poverty-stricken areas in Columbus, Ohio and countless other ministries throughout her Christian walk. While doing a various number of outreach projects she realized her heart was for hurting women. After seeing how God worked in her life, this gave her a desire to help others have an experience like she did.

Lori has been an avid entrepreneur for the past 25 years and loves bringing things to life with her passion and zeal. Lori is the founder of Lori Glaze Ministries.

She loves the outdoors, including fishing, boating and hiking. She also loves exercising, photography and spending time with her family. Lori and her husband, Ryan, have brought together four children. They reside in Grove City, Ohio.

MARY MARY

As the groundbreaking gospel duo, Mary Mary, sisters Erica and Tina Campbell came onto the music scene driven by a fearless and unstoppable creative spirit.

They broke through music barriers in 2000 with their pioneering crossover hit, *"Shackles (Praise You),"* and have since gone on to win numerous accolades.

Erica and Tina Campbell have never wavered from defying convention to fulfill their mission: sending uplifting messages through music and words that are relatable to everyone.

If you would like to purchase the song *Shackles*, you can purchase it on *Amazon.com*.

Coming Soon!
Dispelling the Boogeyman

"The force and fierceness I felt as I drew my hands behind my back knowing I was about to submerge my little seven year-old face into that cold water bobbing for an apple was the most exhilarating thing I had ever experienced. It was like nothing I had ever felt before. There was something drawing every fiber of my being into that moment and made me feel more alive and excited than ever before! This wasn't just a game for me, it was a dark spiritual force that encapsulated my entire being."

CPSIA information can be obtained
at www.ICGtesting.com
Printed in the USA
FFHW011516021019
55347144-61081FF